Wartime St Pancras:

a London borough

defends itself

ISBN 0 904491 64 1

Wartime St Pancras:
a London borough defends itself

Originally compiled by
Charles Allen Newbery

Transcribed & annotated by
Robin Woolven

Edited by
F Peter Woodford

Designed by
Ivor Kamlish

Roll of Honour

Members of the Civil Defence Services killed on duty

Wardens
W J DUNNE
A H NEWTON
C W CATLIN
W E BAPTIST
S BARNETT
L EAST
F THOMPSON

Stretcher Party Leader
F A GRACE

Sewer Foreman
G BUTRESS

Sweeper
W BUTLER

Name listed left	CWGC name	Age	CWGC Information*
W J DUNNE	DUNNE, Walter John	52	Died 9 Oct 40. Air Raid Warden of 37 Tonbridge Houses, died at Cromer Street
A H NEWTON	NEWTON, Alfred Henry	58	Died 15 Oct 40. Air Raid Warden of 8 Caversham Road. Injured at Post 14, Rochester Terrace. Died same day National Temperance Hospital
C W CATLIN	CATLIN, Christopher William	29	Died 17 Apr 41. Air Raid Warden, Firewatcher of 14 Mackeson Rd Hampstead. Died at Chalk Farm Tube Station
W E BAPTIST	BAPTIST, William Edward Charles	68	Died 17 Apr 41. Air Raid Warden, Firewatcher of 71 Jamestown Rd. Died at Tottenham Court Road
S BARNETT	BARNETT, Sidney	35	Died 11 May 41. Air Raid Warden of 14 Mackworth Street. Died at Mackworth Street
L EAST	EAST, Leslie Charles Basil	38	Died 12 May 41. Air Raid Warden, Street Fire Guard of 9 Mackworth Street. Injured 11 May at Mackworth St. Died at University College Hospital
F THOMPSON	THOMSON, Frederick	51	Died 11 May 41. Air Raid Warden. Died at 3 Mackworth Street
F A GRACE	GRACE, Frederick Charles	33	Died 13 May 41. Stretcher Party Leader, Light Rescue Service. Injured 10 May. Died at University College Hospital
G BUTRESS	BUTTRESS, George Frederick	46	Died 17 October 40 at National Temperance Hospital 'due to war operations'. Foreman Flusher (Sewers) of 4 St Anne's Flats, Drummond Street NW1
W BUTLER	BUTLER, David Joseph	42	Died 17 Oct 40 at Dell's Factory, Ryland Road. Municipal Road Sweeper of 18 Grafton Terrace, St Pancras

* CWGC, Commonwealth War Graves Commission

4

Contents

I General Account
by Councillor Newbery

II Service Reports
by Heads of Services

Introduction

by Robin Woolven

With its resident population of some 182,000 citizens and three main-line railway termini, each handling tens of thousands of travellers daily, the Metropolitan Borough of St Pancras was a likely and vulnerable target as war approached in the late 1930s. It was therefore fortunate that amongst its officers and civic leaders, St Pancras had officials who served the borough well in establishing and developing Air Raid Precautions (ARP) to protect the public. Three officers deserving particular mention were the Borough Engineer and Surveyor (Mr C S Bainbridge), the ARP Officer (Major Noel de P MacRoberts) and the sometime Chief Warden (Councillor C Allen Newbery). It was the last-named who compiled this account of how St Pancras prepared for and operated in the Second World War.

London's population had been bombed during the First World War, and people feared the rise of the Fascist powers in Europe and Asia in the 1930s, particularly when they read reports (and saw weekly newsreel films) of the aerial bombardment of civilians by those powers in China, Abyssinia and Spain. When British government policy was finally announced in July 1935, local authorities were made responsible for drawing up plans and for recruiting and training a range of volunteer ARP Services such as First Aid Posts, Rescue and Stretcher Parties, and Decontamination Parties to deal with the expected attacks with poison gas.

Air Raid Wardens were introduced in March 1937. The boroughs were reluctant to spend ratepayers' money on what many considered a government responsibility, so progress with ARP was slow. No central government funding was available until the ARP Act of December 1937 which made provision for block grants for 'authorised' expenditure on local ARP staff and equipment. St Pancras qualified for only a 60% grant for ARP expenditure.

The Council had set up an ARP Committee which first met on 15 September 1936, and the Borough Surveyor and Engineer, Mr Cyril S Bainbridge, was soon tasked with preparing the Borough's ARP Plan. Bainbridge presented his plan, The Battle of London, on 8 March 1937, stressing that it was 'impossible to exaggerate the importance of ARP' and calling for the appointment of a special ARP officer for St Pancras. The War Office promptly supplied a list of 15 suitably qualified persons and, having made a short list of three, the Council appointed Major Noel de Putron MacRoberts DSO MC as ARP Officer on 15 March 1937. He set about organising the recruitment and training of volunteers for the ARP Services. At his own expense in April 1938, MacRoberts visited Spain to observe 'mass terrorism from the air' and, on his return, he published a book[1] noting

---

1 Noel de P MacRoberts *ARP Lessons from Barcelona - Some hints for local authorities and for the private citizen* Eyre & Spottiswoode: London (1938) p.31

that 'a well-organised civil population presents no attraction to enemy air attack – the risks are too great – but a defenceless, unprepared and unorganized city offers a military objective of supreme importance.'

The third officer was Charles Allen Newbery, a 'trimming manufacturer' of 61 Gordon Mansions, Torrington Place, WC1, who appears to have been a latecomer to local government affairs – he was elected to the Council only in October 1937[2] – yet, at the meeting of the ARP Committee on 13 November 1937, he was elected Chairman. This Occasional Paper, produced as a typescript by Newbery in November 1945, takes up the story in some detail from 1937.

At the time, the 60-seat Borough Council was finely balanced, with 33 Municipal Reform (Conservative) and 27 Labour Party members. Only 17 years after the end of 'the war to end all wars', ARP was a politically sensitive matter. Although most people admitted that ARP measures were needed, there was disagreement on what measures were minimally necessary yet adequate, and who should pay for them. Further, many people held pacifist views and were opposed to any ARP measures that might be considered 'warmongering'. Active opposition in the borough came from Communist Party members and sympathisers, led by J B S Haldane (Professor of Biometrics at UCL), who urged the construction of an extensive system of underground tunnels to serve as deep bomb-proof air raid shelters. Haldane's wife, Charlotte, not disclosing her 'secret membership' of the Communist Party, became a Labour Party member of the St Pancras ARP Committee[3], where she joined another journalist and ARP Warden, Miss Barbara Betts (later Baroness Castle), then of 35 Coram Street.[4] In this highly political atmosphere, recruiting for the ARP Services lagged far behind the numbers required, until the September 1938 'Munich' crisis shocked people into the real expectation of war.

Then, gas masks were issued and trench shelters were dug in squares and public open spaces. In this paper Newbery mentions, but does not detail, the extent of trench shelters excavated during the crisis[5]. This work, together with the issue of respirators to (nearly) all of the population, did much to bring home to people the imminence of the coming war. ARP Recruiting was boosted by the crisis and, in May 1939, local authorities were asked to 'so arrange their business that during the next three months priority be given to Civil Defence matters over all other business before them, and to ensure that all responsible officers of the Authorities are instructed accordingly.'

In March 1940 Major MacRoberts was recalled to the Army and was replaced as ARP Officer by Councillor Newbery, who was also by now Chief Warden of St

---

2 As the sixth member, representing the Municipal Reform Party, for the Endsleigh, Whitfield Ward.

3 Charlotte Haldane *Truth Will Out*, The Right Book Club (1949).

4 Baroness Castle *Fighting All the Way* Macmillan (1993). See particularly her Chapter 5.

5 The Government authorised St Pancras to dig 7-ft deep and 5-ft wide trench shelters to accommodate some 23,200 people who might be 'caught in the open' during an air raid. St Pancras was allocated to the public works contractor Messrs. G Percy Trentham Ltd who, by Tuesday 27 September, had over 300 of their own men and another 300 from the Labour Exchange working in Regent's Park (with a mechanical excavator) to provide trenches there for 6,000 people. These trenches were north of Chester Road, as far as Gloucester Gate.

Pancras. Eleven months later, in February 1941, Councillor J E Davies was appointed Chief Warden and ARP Officer and C Allen Newbery was appointed Salvage Officer, to be responsible for the removal, recording and careful storage of furniture from premises damaged by enemy action. Newbery had resigned his Council seat in September 1940 because his ARP duties were keeping him fully occupied, and were likely to increase rather than diminish. So it was as plain Mr C Allen Newbery that he served as Salvage Officer until the end of the war when, banking on his experience successively as chairman of the St Pancras ARP Committee, Chief Warden, ARP Officer and finally Salvage Officer, he collected individual reports in November 1945 from the Heads of all the Civil Defence Services to support and amplify his own chronological narrative. He entitled the whole St Pancras at War.

Such an authoritative memoir of the war 'from the inside' of a London borough is not unique[6] but is nevertheless extremely valuable, for while most reports are brief accounts concentrating on local highlights and incidents, Newbery's account is extensive and supported by details not generally available. For example, the table (p 47) giving the number, capacity and cost of the various types of air raid shelters provided in the borough is, strangely enough, not published anywhere else. Further, Newbery's detailing of the Borough's ARP plans, the range of facilities provided and the Borough

Services deployed during six years of war, together with the individual wartime 'incidents' across St Pancras, will be of great interest to historians and others researching local neighbourhoods.

Although Newbery's paper is detailed and comprehensive, some footnotes have been added either to explain abbreviations, terms or details less familiar to present readers or to amplify or give modern references to events, incidents or locations mentioned in the text. The sketch-map on p 10 has been compiled from one showing Wardens' area boundaries on 2 May 1939; the ARP buildings and facilities shown are based on the information in Newbery's paper. Note the scale of the task which faced the Borough when planning for war and operating under fire.

That the typescript has not previously been published is probably explained by the rapidity with which interest in wartime home-front achievements declined in the post-war years. Even Wing Commander Sir John Hodsoll, the 'father of Civil Defence', the first head of the Home Office ARP Department, who had been involved with ARP matters in Whitehall since 1929, failed to find a publisher for his memoirs[7]. But then, England's remembrance of its successes quickly flags. We publish this paper to place on record the active, efficient preparation and operation of one London borough in defending its population against air attack and the threat of invasion.

---

6 In particular see W Eric Adams 'Civil Defence in Islington (1945), unpublished typescript in Islington Archives and Councillor Sir John Whitty's Progress of the Wardens' Organisation of the City of Westminster (1945), unpublished typescript in Westminster City Archives.

7 Hodsoll's papers, including his draft memoirs, are in the Churchill Archive at Cambridge.

List of illustrations

Map of St Pancras ARP Facilities, 1939-45

A1–A11 Warden Areas, Northern Sector
B1–B12 Warden Areas, Southern Sector

▼ ARP Control and Report Centres
1 Town Hall Basement, Euston Road – South
   Report Centre to March 1942, then whole Borough
2 Electricity Offices, 51 Pratt Street NW1 –
   North Report Centre until closed in March 1942

◆ Headquarters Buildings
3 St Pancras ARP HQ, 72-74 Camden High Street
4 London Region, No.2 Group, North Western
   Polytechnic, Prince of Wales Road, NW5.
   Covering Hampstead, Islington, Paddington,
   St Marylebone, St Pancras and Stoke
   Newington. In 1943 this Group was abolished
   and the boroughs were allocated either to
   Group 1 (Westminster) or Group 3 (The City
   and East End). St Pancras went to Group 1.

● ARP Depots
5 Foster Court, Malet Place WC1
6 Old William Ellis School, Allcroft Road NW5
7 Inverness Street NW1
8 Bartholomew Road NW5
9 Bangor Wharf NW1

■ First Aid Posts
10 Highgate Hospital N6
11 Royal Free Hospital, Gray's Inn Road WC1
12 St Pancras Hospital NW1
13 Elizabeth Garrett Anderson Hospital NW1
14 St Pancras Female Orphanage NW1
15 Outpatients Department,
    Bayham Street NW1
16 St Margaret's Hospital NW5
17 Hampstead General Hospital NW3

▲ Temporary Ambulance Stations
18 Pratt Street NW1
19 102 St Pancras Way NW1
20 20-22 William Road NW1
21 Malden Road NW5
22 St Alban's Road NW5
23 Starcross Street NW1
24 NW Auxiliary, Lawn Road NW3

✦ First-line Rest Centres
25 Mary Ward Centre, Tavistock Place WC1
26 Netley Street School NW1
27 Queen's Crescent school NW5

▲ Miscellaneous
28 ARP Mortuary, Medburn Street, NW1

Part I

General Account

by C Allen Newbery

Abbreviations used in the text
CD   –   Civil Defence
HE   –   high explosive device (bomb)
LCC –   London County Council
MOH –   Borough Medical
             Officer of Health
UXB –   unexploded bomb
WVS –   Women's Voluntary Services

Preparation for war

Notes for this chapter are on pp 15-16

Britain declared war on Germany on 3 September 1939, but its air raid precautions (ARP) began to be organised 4 years earlier. A Home Office circular[1] to local authorities specified the precautionary measures which the Government considered would be necessary for safeguarding the civil population against the effects of air attack. In July 1936, a special (Air Raid Precautions) Committee consisting of 21 members was appointed by St Pancras Borough Council. Councillor Harold Trill was appointed chairman. In February 1937 Major N de P MacRoberts DSO MC & Bar was appointed ARP Officer. The Mayor (Alderman R F W Fincham FCA JP) made a public appeal for volunteers during May 1937 (cf. **[1]**), and by July over 100 citizens had volunteered for duty.

In November, Councillor C Allen Newbery was appointed Chairman of the Special (ARP) Committee. Major N MacRoberts presented a complete scheme for the organisation of the ARP Services in the Borough. During May 1938, the Council decided to purchase the Drill Hall, Camden High Street[2] as ARP Headquarters. During June a survey of air raid shelters was begun. Seven courses of instruction had been drawn up by 400 volunteers, who were presented with the ARP Silver Badge, and by the end of June 140 volunteers had been trained.

Major MacRoberts produced an excellent brochure for factory and business premises which provided a framework for their ARP Schemes, and 1000 copies were distributed throughout the Borough. In July, 23 Head Wardens and their Deputies were interviewed and appointed by the ARP Committee. On 7 September the first floor of Foster Court, Malet Place was taken as a respirator store; on 12 September the Wardens Service commenced, visiting all householders to fit respirators. At the September Council Meeting Mr C S Bainbridge, the Borough Engineer and Surveyor, was relieved of his normal duties and was appointed the responsible officer for the administrative work in connection with ARP, in co-operation with the Medical Officer of Health and the Town Clerk. On 19 September authority was given to place 200,000 respirators in storage at Malet Place[3] and at Old William Ellis School, Allcroft Road. On Sunday 25 September 1938, volunteers assembled 500 respirators at ARP Headquarters.

The Munich crisis

The next morning, 26 September, instructions were received from the Home Office to fit and issue respirators to the public. This information appeared in the midday papers. Only 5000 had so

I Pre-war adjuration to enrol in ARP
Extensive publicity in various media was used to recruit volunteers for the range of ARP Services. Advertisements were displayed in the newspapers, on billboards and on cinema screens while local and national political and civic leaders took every opportunity to appeal to citizens to volunteer.

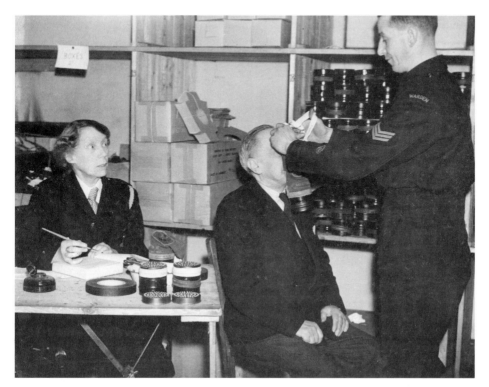

2 Fitting of respirators, ARP HQ, Camden High Street

Civilian gas masks came in three sizes and ARP Wardens had first to carry out a house-to-house check to determine the sizes needed by the people in their area. Cards recording the correct size were issued to citizens and later exchanged for their respirator once the government gave the order. The task of assembling the 200,000 respirators for St Pancras from their component parts (rubber mask and separate filter etc.) was carried out by volunteers during the September 1938 Munich crisis.

far been assembled, so that some rapid arrangements had to be made by Mr Bainbridge. 200 men from the Highways Department were taken off their normal duties, drafted to Malet Place and Old William Ellis School and placed under the direction of Major MacRoberts, the ARP Officer. Chief ARP Instructor Mr P Bettles and his staff worked day and night until the work was completed on Wednesday evening.[4] Eight Fitting Stations were opened by 5 pm and 19 by 9 pm; most members of the public had drawn their respirators by Wednesday afternoon [2]. (During September plans

were approved to use the basement of the new Electricity Offices in Pratt Street[5] as Control Headquarters.

During October and November volunteers continued house-to-house visits to complete the respirator census.[6] The instructional staff at ARP Headquarters was strengthened, and classes for volunteers were held on 5 nights a week; arrangements were also made to start a special course to train certain volunteers as local instructors to gain their LARP Certificate. On 21 December 1938 a Mr H G May offered to organise the Rescue and Demolition Parties.

On 1 January 1939, 128 men were enrolled for First Aid Parties (Stretcher), and 73 men and 231 women for First Aid Posts. A complete report was presented by Mr R C Coss, First Engineering Assistant, on the organisation of the decontamination and road repair services; Mr R C Hay was recruited from the building trade in the Borough. During March, eight First Aid Posts were approved, and Councillor Newbery was appointed Chief Warden. At the Council Meeting of 3 May 1939[7], the following resolutions were approved:

That Mr C S Bainbridge, Borough Engineer & Surveyor, be appointed ARP Controller[8] for the Borough, with authority to exercise such powers as may be necessary to carry out the requirements of the Government in matters related to Civil Defence, in the event of a national emergency arising.

That the Council do appoint an Air Raid Precautions Emergency Committee consisting of three members of the Council to act in co-operation with the ARP Controller.

That the Town Clerk be appointed Co-ordinating Officer.

That Mr G S E Barker, Deputy Borough Engineer & Surveyor, be designated 'ARP Organiser', that he be required to devote the whole of his time to the organisation and supervision of the technical staff, working squads and the Wardens Service.

Provisional Local War Instructions were received giving full details on what action to be taken in the event of an outbreak of hostilities. On 14 June Dr J H Briscoe-Smith was appointed ARP Medical Officer, to be responsible to the Medical Officer of Health for the organisation and training of First Aid (Stretcher) Parties and First Aid Posts.

Councillor Newbery called a meeting of funeral directors in the Borough to discuss how they could co-operate with the Mortuary Superintendent. During June and July the Chief Warden, together with Mr G S Jopling, Engineering Assistant, visited New Scotland Yard for conferences with the Hon. Arthur Howard,[9] Principal Air Raid Warden for London, regarding the number of Wardens' Posts required. In view of the large amount of railway property in the Borough the original number of 33 was increased to 37.

From September 1938 onwards the provision of shelter accommodation against air attack was a constant problem. Every possible avenue was explored, and various schemes were put into operation.

3 Control Room, Town Hall, Euston Road
Originally, the St Pancras Northern Control Room was in the former Electricity Department in Pratt Street, Southern Control in the basement of the Town Hall. In 1942, the Pratt Street Control was closed and the whole borough was then controlled from the Town Hall.

For a full report, see p 46.

In July specific instructions about Civil Defence were issued nationally. On 23 August, instructions were received from the police to man the telephones in the Control Room. On 26 August, a meeting was held in the North Control Room at Pratt Street, attended by all chief officers, Mr C S Bainbridge in the Chair. Progress and organisation of the various services were reviewed. The general co-ordinated action of each service in the event of an air raid was agreed. Mr Bainbridge and Mr Robert Lee were to take charge of operational duties in the Control Room on alternate 24-hour shifts, and Mr G S E Barker and Mr W C W Roworth to perform the same duties at the South Report Centre, Town Hall [3].

On Thursday 31 August, messages arrived with the code word LEWIN – what did it mean? The answer was in the Town Clerk's safe, where the Provisional Local War Instructions had rested since March. They were handed out to Heads of Services and gave elaborate and complicated instructions for the calling up of all services on the day when they had to be put into operation. These instructions were followed and personnel began to report at the various depots and wardens' posts on the same day. Some days afterwards, when some officers were comparing notes with other Boroughs, it was discovered that some Authorities had called up too many people.

On mobilisation, conditions at the depots were poor, no proper sleeping accommodation or canteens had been provided. It was necessary at Inverness Street and Bartholomew Road Depots to erect temporary quarters formed with timber and sandbags and fitted with rough bunks. Some men slept in their lorries (if only these lorries could speak, what a tale they could tell!) and some on their stretchers. Meals were taken at local dining rooms, no canteen facilities being available at any depot. Conditions were soon improved, sleeping accommodation was found at Old William Ellis School and Malet Place Depots, men from Bartholmew Road Depot slept at Torriano Road Schools and from Inverness Street at Hawley Road Schools. Canteens were soon arranged by the Borough Treasurer (Mr C Davey), Mr A W Martin being appointed Canteen Manager.

The Stretcher Parties, with Dr J H Briscoe-Smith as Officer-in Charge, assisted by Mr E T Milburn (who had been instructing in First Aid since 1938), shared these Depots with the Rescue Service and Demolition squads, organised by the London County Council, with Mr H E Watkinson, District Surveyor for North St Pancras, as Officer-in-Charge, supported by London County Council clerks of works at each depot. Until Depot Superintendents were appointed, the senior Sanitary Inspectors carried out these duties and assisted in getting order out of chaos. All ranks were keen and did their best to settle down to a new life under difficult conditions; a new life in which it was expected that poison gas might play a large part [4, p 16].

A Depot Superintendent appointed by the Council was responsible to the Controller for fatigue parties and cleanliness at the Depots. It was not an easy job to run a Depot consisting of two different services under different authorities, each service having different equipment and different types of bunks and bedding, the latter causing many arguments and squabbles, which continued for years.

Notes

1 The Home Office Circular allocating responsibilities to local authorities (on sale to the public for 2d) was issued on 9 July 1935. Newbery became actively involved in November 1937, just as the ARP Act providing central government block grants for authorised ARP expenditure was about to be passed by Parliament.

2 At 72-76 Camden High Street. In 2005 this was a branch of *Argos*, having been a *Kwik Save* supermarket for decades.

3 Now part of University College, on the right hand side of the alley across Tavistock Place from the north end of Malet Street.

4 As well as assembling and issuing 167,000 gas masks to St Pancras citizens during the crisis, these men dug miles of shallow (7 ft deep) trench shelters in parks and squares as air raid shelters. ('Anderson' and surface shelters were not provided until early in 1939.) Most of the trenches were later provided with covers, duck-boards, concrete linings, lighting and (very limited) sanitation.

(contd on p 16)

4 Gas Cleansing Station, King's Cross Coach station, undressing room
The decontamination of people subject to a poison gas attack was to be dealt with by first removing their contaminated clothing and putting it in the dustbin shown, then cleansing their bodies with water in a separate shower room. Fresh clothing was then to be issued and the people would be able to return to their duties or homes.

Notes contd.

5 The Electricity Offices were at 51 Pratt Street NW1, in 2005 the site of a block of flats on the south western corner of the junction with Camden Street.

6 The census was to determine the remaining requirements for adult respirators – the distribution of respirators for children started some time later.

7 In May 1939, the ARP Department of the Home Office requested all London local authorities to give civil defence matters top priority.

8 The position of Air Raid Controller was an important one, to be filled by a competent officer (generally the Town Clerk) and not an elected member. In an emergency, the Controller was responsible to the Regional Authorities, not his local authority. Outside London the post of Controller was often given to Chief Constables, but it was not appropriate for the Commissioner of the Metropolitan Police (Air Vice-Marshal Sir Phillip Game) to control the City and 28 Metropolitan Boroughs.

9 MP for St George's Division of Westminster 1945-50. A son-in-law of Rt Hon. Stanley Baldwin.

St Pancras ARP Organisation on 3 September 1939

Controller
Mr C S Bainbridge,
AMICE, PASI, MIM & CYE,
Borough Engineer &
Surveyor

Deputy Controller
Mr W C W Roworth,
Administrative Officer,
Estates Department

ARP Organiser
Mr G S E Barker
AMICE, MIM. & CYE,
Dep Borough Engineer
& Surveyor

ARP Officer
Major N MacRoberts
DSO, MC

Chief Warden
Councillor C Allen Newbery

Deputy Chief Warden
Councillor John E Davies

Medical Services

Dr Maitland-Radford
MD, BS, DPH
Medical Officer of Health

Dr J H Briscoe-Smith
ARP MO - Stretcher Party
Service and First Aid Posts

Mr D Crozier
Superintendent of
Mortuaries

Mr H E Watkinson
Rescue Service and
Demolition

Mr R C Coss
AMIM CYE PASI
Decontamination Officer

Mr A W Davey AMCHE
Transport Officer

Mr S Jacobs
Gas Detection Officer

**Control Room,
Electricity Offices,
Pratt Street**
O/Cs alternate nights
Mr C S Bainbridge
and Mr R Lee

**South Report Centre,
The Town Hall**
O/Cs alternate nights
Mr W C W Roworth
and Mr G S E Barker

Depots

Old William Ellis School,
Bartholomew Road,
Inverness Street,
Malet Place

Outbreak of war

Notes on this chapter are on p 21

Great Britain declared war on Germany on Sunday 3 September 1939. The broadcast announcement by the Prime Minister, Mr Neville Chamberlain, was immediately followed by the Warning Signal given on the sirens. The Control Room, Report Centres, 37 Wardens' Posts, 8 First Aid Posts and 4 ARP Depots were all manned and ready for what was to come.[10] The information available before the war led us to believe that bombing would cause very heavy casualties, and arrangements had been made to deal with them.

On Monday 4 September, the ARP Special Emergency Committee[11] held its first meeting. The Committee was presided over by the Mayor, Councillor G A Watts JP; other Committee members were Alderman Sir David Davies, Councillor F W Powe JP LCC, the Controller (Mr C S Bainbridge), Mr A Powell-Coke as Co-ordinating Officer and Dr Maitland-Radford, MOH. The Committee faced a formidable task, including carrying out the following Home Office instructions: enforcing lighting restrictions, completing the issue of respirators, protection of important buildings, provision of shelters, equipping the First Aid Posts, calling up paid workers and part-time volunteers, and organising the Report & Control Centre.

The previous night, the Controller, the Chief Warden, the MOH and representatives of other services had slept at the Control Room, Pratt Street, accommodation being arranged in different offices; beds had to be set up at night and taken down the following morning. At the South Report Centre the staff slept in various parts of the Town Hall, some of the more fortunate ones on settees outside the Council Chamber; Mr W C W Roworth and Mr G S E Barker were Officer-in-Charge on alternate nights.

The eight First Aid Posts were stationed at Highgate Hospital, Royal Free

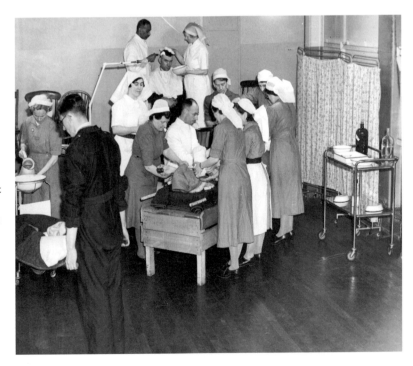

5 St Margaret's First Aid Post, Leighton Road
This was one of the eight First Aid Posts established at the hospitals across the Borough. Many more Posts were originally set up but once it was found that the number of casualties was far less than had been predicted, the facilities were concentrated in the Borough's hospitals.

Hospital[12], St Pancras Hospital, Elizabeth Garrett Anderson Hospital, St Pancras Female Orphanage, Hampstead General Hospital, the Out-Patients Department, Bayham Street, and St Margaret's Hospital, Leighton Road **[5]**.

Personnel had been trained and each Post had the services of three or four doctors. There were, in addition, two Mobile First Aid posts, one stationed at Highgate Hospital and the other at St Margaret's Hospital. Eight Ambulance Stations served the Borough and were under the control of the LCC, but under operational control in the Borough.

The Wardens' Service was controlled by the Chief Warden (Councillor Newbery), stationed at ARP Headquarters, Camden High Street, who was responsible for organisation and training to the Hon. Arthur Howard, Principal Air Raid Warden for London. The 37 Wardens' Posts were divided into four districts, each under a District Warden. During the early days of the war, a large number of people enrolled in the Wardens' Service, bringing the strength to more than 700 paid Wardens. This number had to be reduced to 450 paid personnel. Men received £3 a week and women £2 a week. All the original Post Wardens were well known in their area; they had to get to know not only their own personnel but to know and gain the confidence of all who lived in their area.

The Control Room and Report Centre at Pratt Street and South Report Centre at the Town Hall were manned by volunteers from the Electrical Department, Pratt Street, and Town Hall staff, who volunteered for this work before the outbreak of war. They took on this duty during the first few weeks throughout 24 hours, but as bombing did not materialise, more paid staff were employed to operate the telephones during office hours, the volunteer staff being on the premises if required.

During March 1940 Major MacRoberts, the ARP Officer, was recalled to the Army and resigned his position on the Council. Major MacRoberts had been appointed in March 1937, and did excellent work in the training of volunteers before and during the war, as well as preparing the combined training exercises and so on. He was succeeded as ARP Officer by Councillor Newbery; Councillor J E Davies, Deputy

Chief Warden was promoted to Chief Warden, and Councillor J A Wright was appointed Deputy Chief Warden.

Between 5 pm and 6 pm on Saturday 7 September 1940, the first heavy air raid on London took place. The attack, which was repeated at 8 pm, was aimed at the East End and Docklands, where fires started in the afternoon lighted the target.[13]

Although no bombs fell on St Pancras, we were asked to send twelve ambulances, five sitting cars and four heavy rescue parties to Docklands, but their rendezvous point was destroyed before their arrival, the entire area being blocked by debris and fires; some streets were running with tar, the parties never reached their destination, and it took weeks to remove the tar from some of the vehicles.

On Sunday 8 September, the first bombs fell on St Pancras at 10.20 pm, demolishing houses in Hargrave Terrace, Bartholomew Road and Busby Place; a few hours later, at 3.35 am a high-explosive (HE) bomb fell on the east side of Harrington Square, at the junction of Hampstead Road, demolishing three houses and badly damaging many more, a large crater occupying the full width of the carriageway, and a portion of the trenches in Harrington Square also being damaged. A London Passenger Transport bus was thrown up against one of the houses with the front of the bus resting on the first floor level, the occupants of the bus having just taken cover in the trench shelter **[6, p 20]**.

This proved to be a very stern test for the Rescue and Stretcher Parties, going into action for the first time. Two members of the Rescue Service received the George Medal for their gallantry in their work at this incident: **R D STEWART** for "outstanding courage and disregard for personal safety in efforts to release dead and injured people from a vault shelter; a bus had been thrown end up against this house, the near end crashing through pavement. He rescued two live casualties, working under the bus, which may have crashed on him at any moment." and **A G PALMER**, who "crawled under a mass of debris, which was in danger of collapse, to shield a female casualty from falling debris, and remained with her for over three hours. This was the first incident on which his party had been engaged."

Valuable assistance was also rendered by Alderman Dr Greig, who assisted the ARP Services. 11 people were killed, 6 seriously injured and a number of minor injuries were dealt with at the First Aid Post.

About an hour later another HE bomb fell in Allcroft Road, which smashed an Anderson shelter containing a number of people, badly damaged a number of houses and blasted a large area. This happened almost outside the Depot at Old William Ellis School. The parties got on with the rescue work as soon as soon as the bomb fell without waiting for orders from Control. In this very unpleasant incident, the killed and injured were known to the Depot personnel; a number of the injured were taken into the depot for First Aid treatment, where the Mobile Medical Unit also attended. 16 persons were killed, 3 seriously injured and 42 slightly injured. The rescue work was well done, and proved the value of their training.

6 Bombed bus in Harrington Square

The first bombs to fall in St Pancras, on 8 September 1940, included that on Harrington Square NW1 where this London bus was blown onto the houses - its driver and passengers having taken refuge in the trench shelters in Harrington Square.

The St Pancras ARP Services survived their first trial of strength with distinction. The Wardens' Service and Control functioned well. Our front-line period of service had begun. The Rest Centre organisation, controlled by the London County Council, operated well and proved adequate for the task; Queens Crescent and Netley Street Rest Centres were opened.

The HE bomb in Argyle Street, at the corner of Birkenhead Street, also caused a nasty incident; here some casualties were rescued alive 12 hours later.

The ARP Depots were working 24-hour shifts, the changeover taking place at 8 am; on Monday morning the new shifts took over from those who had been working most of the night and carried on with the rescue work. That night saw bombs fall in Argyle Street, Guilford Street, Frederick Street and Byron Court, Mecklenburgh Square. Byron Court was a hostel for women, containing a large number of furnished rooms on five

After this incident two members of the Rescue Squad were awarded George Medals for their heroism in rescuing people from the debris. This photograph and films taken of the incident were given much publicity, especially in America, by the Ministry of Information to show the results of German bombing.

floors. Fires broke out in the middle of the building and there was also considerable flooding in the basement; about the same time an unexploded bomb (UXB) fell on the trench shelter in the Square and an HE fractured the gas main in Guilford Street which caught fire; the Fire Brigade had to spray water on the houses on both sides of the street to prevent their catching fire. At Byron Court, 4 people were killed, 3 seriously injured and 15 slightly injured. Many static water tanks were constructed to provide readily accessible water to the Fire Service, for example the one off Gordon Square, in the grounds of University College [7].

10 The feared German 'knockout blow' against London did not materialise, in fact no bombs fell on London for nearly a year and this valuable lull was used to better equip, train and exercise the range of ARP Services.

11 To facilitate effective local government in wartime, local authorities were instructed to nominate a small (ideally, 3-person) Emergency Committee with whom (not to whom) the ARP Controller would work. The size limitation was relaxed later in the war.

12 Then in Gray's Inn Road, now the site of the Eastman Dental Hospital.

13 This day was dubbed 'Black Saturday', the start of the main Blitz, when hundreds of people in the East End dockland areas of Poplar, West Ham and other riverside boroughs were killed and many more seriously injured. Mutual support arrangements ensured that the hard-pressed ARP and Fire Services in Docklands were reinforced by men and equipment from other Groups in London and other Regions.

7 Static water tank, Gordon Street, Bloomsbury

Bomb damage caused this extensive gap in the terrace on the west side of Gordon Street. It was used, in part, to accommodate a large Static Water tank – storing water for use by the firefighters in the event of further raiding (the damaged dome of University College in the background). The right-hand side of the site is now occupied by the Bloomsbury Theatre.

The Blitz

Notes on this chapter are on p 27

On 18 September 1940 a parachute mine exploded in the middle of Euston Road, outside the Potato Market, causing very few casualties but doing tremendous blast damage to Clifton House, the Euston Cinema, Euston Tavern and the north and west sides of the Town Hall, the offices in the north-west corner taking most of the blast. There was damage also in Ossulston Street, Chalton Street, Judd Street, Bidborough Street and Euston Road.

An unexploded bomb (UXB) was reported in a house in Harrington Square which on examination proved to be an unexploded parachute mine, the first we had seen. The silk cords of the parachute were neatly wrapped around each chimney of the stack. The mine measured 8 ft 6 inches by 2 ft 2 inches in diameter, passing through the roof, one end of the attic, down through the next floor and peeping through the ceiling below.

A Naval Party arrived and made the mine 90% safe. The RSD (Rescue Service and Demolition) Squads were asked to remove it to safety. This proved to be a big job, a way had to be cut through the floors and the mine very gently lowered to the ground floor, then an opening made in the front wall to get it onto the pavement for loading up. Mr T Boulter, Clerk of Works, RSD Squads assisted by Mr J Freedman, Engineer Assistant, supervised its removal from the building and loaded it on to a Highways Department lorry, taking it to the Inner Circle, Regent's Park where it rested the night. The following day the Bomb Disposal Squads removed the mine to Hackney Marshes where it was blown up. This first experience in handling an unexploded parachute mine was a valuable lesson for Mr Freedman, who soon had to deal with many types of unexploded bombs and mines. The specimen was quite a show exhibit, and many people went to view it; one man even photographed it, which at a much later date nearly got him into serious trouble.

At this early stage of bombing, very few Bomb Disposal Squads were available in London. During September 1940 any suspected unexploded bomb reported in the borough (including on railway property) meant that the Engineering Assistant on duty, or the ARP Officer, was asked by Control to go out and investigate whether a bomb had actually fallen, and failed to explode or penetrated deeply and exploded underground. Control passed his report on to Group 2, and if it was confirmed the Bomb Disposal Officer arranged for it to be removed. The Council officers, who had no guidance on this kind of bomb, had to use their own common sense and powers of observation. Excellent work was carried out by Messrs G Dale, C Jopling, W Beesley, J Freedman, G Wilkinson and J Sutton: they did their bomb reconnaissance work as a voluntary duty and gave no thought to their personal safety and regardless of the fact that they were not covered by any special insurance scheme. If a suspected UXB was confirmed, all buildings in the area had to be evacuated by the occupiers and the road was closed to all traffic.

A year before this, no bomb disposal squads were in existence, and it was not until February 1940 that the Royal Engineers were asked to form Bomb Disposal Squads. They had very little information to work on and no special tools to work with; during the early days of the bombing many Squad members were killed. A special system of categories were arranged, and only those bombs in Category A were removed at once. The categories were recommended by the Controller and then had to be confirmed by London Region, who instructed the Bomb Disposal Officer as to the order of priority. The greatest number of UXBs at one time was 16 on the night of 18/19 September 1940, and 20 on the night of 27/28 September 1940.

On the afternoon of 20 September, 3 small bombs fell near Tottenham Court Road, no warning having been sounded. One bomb fell in Euston Road near the Wellcome Institute, which caused some flooding; one bomb fell in Maple's furniture store but failed to explode; the third fell on the pavement of Howland Street outside the Langham Telephone Exchange, causing a lot of damage to the basement. Had the warning been sounded the basement would have been full of telephone operators.

On the night of 16/17 September, 10 HEs were dropped, the main incident being at St Pancras Hospital, where the receiving ward was destroyed. All patients were evacuated from A Block to H and I Blocks; a UXB fell in the Mental Ward; the Stretcher Parties and the Ambulances, assisted by the Hospital Staff, evacuated 130 patients.

On the evening of the 20th a very nasty incident was caused outside King's Cross Station, when an AA shell struck the pavement outside a small café, causing the death of 17 people and injuries to 14.

The night of the 24th was a bad one for the southern end of the Borough, when a parachute mine exploded in Tottenham Court Road outside the YMCA causing a 28 ft crater. A public house[14], a funfair and many shops were destroyed, and there were heavy casualties. A bomb also fell on St Pancras Hospital, with considerable damage but few casualties. Incendiary bombs set three large fires, the London University Library was destroyed, Maple's in Tottenham Court Road and Oetzmann's in Hampstead Road were seriously damaged.

On the 25th a parachute mine fell in Highgate Road by St Albans Road, demolishing a number of houses and causing blast damage in Highgate Road, St Albans Road, Brookfield Park and Swains Lane.

On the night of 27/28 September, 21 HEs fell in Kentish Town: 16 of them in the Post 9 area. 3 flats were destroyed in Camelot House, killing three people and injuring 19. The entrance of the North West Polytechnic, Prince of Wales Road was damaged: the Group 2 Headquarters[15] in the basement was shaken up but there were no casualties. A large number of shops were blasted in Kentish Town Road and the road was covered in broken glass for a considerable distance, but the Road Repair Parties had this cleared away in record time.

The early part of October was fairly quiet until the 15th, when a number of parachute mines fell in the southern end of the Borough. Great damage was done at Prospect Terrace, Cromer Street and St Pancras Station. The first PM exploded in Cromer Street at 3.15 am demolishing a large number of houses and shops and causing heavy blast damage in Argyle Street, Harrison Street and surrounding district; 8 people were killed, a number injured and a large number rendered homeless. At 3.50 am Prospect Terrace flats were hit, half of them were demolished and 30 people were killed. Prospect Terrace was a solid brick structure which, when collapsed, made rescue work very slow and difficult; rescue work continued until 3 November. Damage was also done to Fiona House and property in Heathcote Street.

A third mine got caught in the Signal Box at the end of No.1 platform of the station; this did not explode until a few hours later. The station had been cleared and no casualties were caused, although there was considerable damage to the station, and a lot of debris fell in Midland Road.

An unexploded PM landed at 285 Gray's Inn Road, next door to the Royal Free Hospital, which had to be evacuated; Frederick Street, Acton Street, Albert Street, Little Edward Street and Albany Street had to be cleared. These four unexploded PMs caused hundreds of people to be evacuated in addition to those rendered homeless. The same night an HE bomb hit Camden Town Tube Station, but did not seriously damage it [8, p 24].

Bombing continued to be heavy until the end of the month. On the evening of 16 October 1940, Sewer Foreman G Buttress was killed by enemy action whilst on duty in Warren Street. Serious damage was done when a large HE bomb fell in Eversholt Street at the junction of Phoenix Road, penetrating the Hampstead Tube Line, blocking the South Tunnel and flooding the North Tunnel; all services in Eversholt Street were interrupted and Mornington Crescent Tube Station was closed for some months.

Early in November St Pancras Station was again damaged. At 10 am one Saturday morning 4 HEs were dropped at King's Cross Goods Station. 20 people were killed, 32 seriously injured and 50 slightly injured. The LNER [London and North Eastern Railway] immediately asked Control for assistance; rescue parties and a large number of ambulances, together with an Incident Officer, were sent. Rescue work was hampered by the large number of workmen who wanted to help, but they soon gave way when the Incident Officer took over.

During this period one small incident caused a large headache for the Control Room. A bomb damaged some houses and killed a donkey, all casualties were safely removed and the incident was closed, but the dead donkey remained. The weather was warm, days passed by, the Wardens got worried and kept pestering Control. It was certainly not a job for the Stretcher Parties; nothing to do with the Heavy Rescue Service; as it was not in the highway, the Highways Department was not responsible. So after a lot of bother, this poor inoffensive but offensive animal was removed by the police.

At this stage all the ARP Services had

settled down, and their early training proved sound and practical. The Wardens did wonderful work and were very keen; the women Wardens did their job as well as any man. Some Wardens were killed on duty in Cromer Street and Kentish Town. The Stretcher Party and Ambulance Service worked well together; the Heavy Rescue Service tackled any job that came along and worked under conditions that were much improved at a later date.

During October regulations were received giving particulars of two new awards for civilian bravery – the George Cross and the George Medal, the George Cross being the civilian equivalent to the Victoria Cross. Most large incidents produced many acts of gallantry, when all services went out to get on with the job and innumerable acts of bravery took place, which made it invidious to recommend particular persons for the

8 Camden Town Station after bombing
The presence of an upright No.24 bus adds to the normality of this 'business as usual' scene. Obviously, no indication appears in this picture of the 8000-place 'Deep Shelter' excavated beneath the Northern Line tunnels at the station and opened to the public in July 1944.

coveted award. Full particulars of Honours and Awards given to the Civil Defence[16] Services will be found on p 89.

January 1941 saw a number of small raids. One afternoon at 3.45 pm three bombs fell near Lismore Circus, one of them in Oakfield Crescent, near a site which was being cleared by the Pioneer Corps, 10 of whose members were killed and 1 taken to hospital. On the evening of the 11th a stick of bombs dropped near St Pancras Way by Georgiana Street, one falling down a boiler flue in St Pancras Borough Council Power Station, exploding in the gas-washing tank, the second striking the canal pump house, blowing out 400 feet of wall, wrecking the pump house and fracturing a 36-inch main.

On the night of the 17th all was quiet; soon after midnight, the all-clear had been sounded and the voluntary Control Room Shift returned to bed. At 1.50 am a large explosion shook the Town Hall and there was a general rush to the Control Room. One officer on duty thought the Town Hall had been hit and ran upstairs in dressing gown and pyjamas to see whether the Town Hall Guard was all right. The Guard was well but a little shaky; he stated that the bomb fell outside, but ... close. On going outside to investigate, the officer fell over a large piece of iron from the roof of the Euston Cinema, where the bomb had fallen on the rear portion, doing blast damage in Bidborough Street. A second bomb fell at the same time on the back of the Kentish Arms, demolishing the staircase and saloon bar. Councillor Blackmoor and his wife, who were unhurt but trapped upstairs, made their escape down a fire ladder.

Soon after the bomb dropped the warning was sounded. This was the only occasion when St Pancras had its own private raid, as no other bombs were dropped on London that night.

On 28 January 1941, the Civil Defence Comforts Fund came into being. "Bundles for Britain" arrived from the Colonies containing scarves, socks, oiled stockings, pullovers, gloves, wristlets, Balaclava helmets, etc. for distribution to the Forces and Civil Defence Services. Many articles contained notes containing good-luck messages and the names and addresses of the senders. These gifts were keenly sought after. An appeal was made by the Mayor to raise funds for buying wool, to be knitted into garments by parties of ladies organised by the WVS.

At 1.15 pm an HE bomb fell on a grocery store in the Hampstead Road demolishing the shop; fire broke out, which was dealt with by the Fire Brigade. 10 people were killed and 9 injured. A man was trapped beneath burning and unstable debris, surmounted by an apparently unstable 3-storey building; Stretcher Party Leader J O'Sullivan went in under the debris in an attempt to save the man, but was forced to come out by the spreading fire and smoke. He reported that the man was still alive. Stretcher Party Instructor W J Smaje subsequently made further attempts, while the fire was still burning and when it was known that the large paraffin tank was likely to explode at any moment. He succeeded in reaching the man, and only gave up his efforts to release the casualty when he collapsed from partial asphyxiation. For this great effort Smaje was awarded the George Medal and O'Sullivan received a Commendation (p 89).

During February the ARP Committee reorganised certain positions in the ARP Service. Chief Warden Cllr J E Davies was appointed Chief Warden and ARP Officer, with responsibility for organisation of the Wardens' Service, supervision of air raid shelters, enforcement of the Fire Guard order and supervision of ARP Depots. Mr C A Newbery was appointed Salvage Officer, responsible for the collection, removal and storage of furniture from premises damaged by enemy action.

March was a fairly quiet month, but on the 29th a parachute mine fell outside Datchet House: 3 were killed, 7 seriously injured and 8 slightly injured. Only the end of one block was seriously damaged, but had it fallen on the flats or in one of the courtyards, the position would have been very different.

The night of 16/17 April 1941[17] will always be remembered by Londoners, those in St Pancras particularly, as one of the heaviest raids on London. 15 HEs, 5 parachute mines, 2 unexploded bombs and hundreds of incendiary bombs fell, causing over 50 incidents The raid began with an AA shell falling in Prince of Wales Road about 9.30, then things were fairly quiet until about midnight, when bombing got into full swing and continued until daybreak.

No. 3 Shift with the Deputy Controller W C W Roworth in charge, worked steadily from midnight until 9.30 am. A total of 208 people were killed during the raid. The biggest incident was caused by a parachute mine falling in the courtyard next to the surface shelter of a block of working-class flats built in 1841 in St Pancras Square. A large portion of the flats was demolished, and there was severe damage in Pratt Street, Pancras Road and the surrounding area. 78 people were killed, 58 were taken to hospital and there were 40 minor casualties. Because of the heavy raid in progress, the seriousness of this incident was not appreciated until the morning, when rescue work proved a big problem, as rescue parties had to work near dangerous walls that might collapse at any moment. 70 Royal Engineers assisted in the removal of debris; a mobile crane was provided by the London and North Eastern Railway. In several cases 4 or 5 members of a family were killed. The Incident Officers had to deal with hundreds of queries from parents and relatives. The Salvage Officer removed six lorry-loads of clothing, bedding and small articles of furniture collected from the street.

Another mine also fell on the north-west wing of Montague Tibbles House, a modern block of Council flats; flats fronting on Queens Crescent were severely damaged; 16 people were killed and 8 taken to hospital.

Bombs also fell at the corner of Craddock Street and Prince of Wales Road, which blasted the façade of Montague Tibbles House. Parachute mines fell in Oakley Square and Leeke Street, the latter damaging the Metropolitan Railway outside King's Cross Station, seriously damaging the bridge. St Pancras Hospital was also hit: the First Aid post was put out of action but was re-established at the Royal Veterinary College. A bad fire occurred at Malet Place, doing severe damage to the Library; the Depot personnel worked hard to fight the fire, but very few men were left at the depot and they failed in their attempts. No serious damage was done to the Depot stores. A number of bombs fell in Maple's in Tottenham Court Road and in the Express Dairy building in Tavistock Place. Damage was also done at Haverstock Hill, Crogsland Road, Bath Row, Aldenham Street, Maple Street, Diana Place, Euston Road, Howland Mews, Tottenham Court Road, Acton Street, Stanley Buildings, Gray's Inn Road and the British Medical Association Building, Tavistock Place.

On the night of 10/11 May the heaviest raid on London took place of which St Pancras received its full share: 52 HEs, 1 PM, 9 UXBs and hundreds of incendiary bombs. The fires were so numerous it was impossible for the Fire Brigade to deal with even half of them; great work in this direction was done by fire guard parties, fire watchers and householders.

A new feature of this raid was pattern bombing: in a small area between Goodge Street and Tottenham Street seven HE bombs were dropped, some of them so close together that Control thought that some incidents had been reported twice. During the raid 84 people were killed – a small number considering the number of incidents and damage done. The Charlotte Street group of bombs is a good example of pattern bombing. One fell on the west corner of Charlotte Street and Goodge Street, two houses were on fire on the east side of Charlotte facing the bomb damage, 50 yards up Charlotte Street two HEs fell close together in the middle of the road, fracturing the water main and causing considerable flooding; a Public House received a direct hit at the corner of Scala Street and Charlotte Street; six houses were demolished at the corner of Tottenham Street and Charlotte Street, including a jeweller's shop (which incidentally recovered most of its goods); a further HE and a UXB fell in Chitty Street. The UXB severed a gas main, starting a fire in a public shelter next door, which was hurriedly evacuated. All this packet of trouble took place in Wardens' Post 37 Area, which kept Post Warden Murray very busy.

Incidents also took place near Fitzroy Square: 2 HEs Fitzroy Street, 1 HE Fitzroy Place, 1 HE Conway Street, 1 HE Maple Street and 1 HE Maple Place.

The next group was on the stations: 3 HE bombs fell on St Pancras Station, one between No. 3 & 4 platforms at the point where the lines terminated, and penetrated the vaults below. Another fell in Euston Road, outside Clifton House, striking a Metropolitan train in the tunnel underneath the road, also doing heavy damage, for the second time, to Clifton House, Euston Tavern, St Pancras Town Hall and surrounding property.

Still another fell at the corner of Dukes Road and Euston Road, smashing a petrol station and damaging the flats in Dukes Road. A number of Pioneers were hastily sent for to assist in removing the petrol, for fear of it getting into the sewers and causing an explosion. Another fell on Levita House (an LCC block of flats in Ossulston Street) doing much damage.

Another group spread from Endsleigh Gardens to Tottenham Court Road. A Public House in Gower Place, the Hawarden Castle, was demolished; the 'Castle' was frequently patronised by members of the Free French Forces who lived at General de Gaulle's headquarters at the London School of Tropical Medicine, which was also badly damaged and had to be evacuated. Damage was also done in Endsleigh Street and to the University of London buildings, and bad fires occurred in Torrington Place, Huntley Street, New Inn Yard and Tottenham Court Road. The railway bridge in Hampstead Road was also damaged, as were Harrington Street (2 HEs), Netley Street, Mackworth Street,[18] Mornington Street, Albert Street, Cumberland Market and Arlington Road. The Gray's Inn Road district received damage in Gray's Inn Road itself, Pakenham Street, Calthorpe Street, Guildford [sic] Street, Bernard Street and Phoenix Place (1 HE , 1 UXB). Kentish Town had its share, with damage at Willes Road, Haverstock Hill (1 HE), Wellesley Road and Queens Crescent.

In the north of the Borough 3 HEs fell in Brecknock Road, two direct hits which also caused damage in Lupton Street, one in the middle of Brecknock Road which fractured two 36-inch trunk water mains from the reservoir which supplied the City, and completely blocked Brecknock Road to all traffic. Two bombs fell in Fortress Road and there was damage in Brookfield Park; 1 HE in Highgate Road and 3 HEs on Parliament Hill Fields.

A few days later the Salvage Officer was handed an iron stewing pan that had been found in the garden of a demolished house; the Golden Syrup tins inside it contained 399 £1 notes. Thus there are some honest people about who do hand valuables in.

About 5 a.m. a report was received from Euston Station of a strange smell which was suspected as poison gas. Two members of No 3 Shift went to investigate (taking respirators but no protective clothing); after climbing down hundreds of steps they found an incendiary bomb which had been well doused with water, giving off a kind of acetylene smell. Thank goodness, that was the only time poison gas was reported.

The All Clear was sounded about 6 a.m. on 17 April 1941, a beautiful clear morning, with hundreds of fires reflected in the sky.

This proved to be the end of the Blitz on London. It was an experience never to be forgotten, a wonderful experience for the Civil Defence Services – who in spite of the difficulties and dangers did a real job of work and were proud and privileged to do it. The Blitz helped London to find its soul; taught a real feeling of comradeship and how to make friends with one's neighbours. A wonderful spirit bred during danger – to be continued, we hope, in the peaceful days to come.

Notes

14 The Blue Posts public house on Tottenham Court Road.

15 For operational control and mutual support, the City and the 28 Metropolitan Boroughs of Inner London were divided into five Groups. St Pancras was part of Group 2, with its HQ in Prince of Wales Road. After the main Blitz, Group 2 was abolished to save manpower, and its Boroughs were reallocated between Group 1 (Westminster) and Group 3 (The City and East End). St Pancras was allocated to Group 1 which is why, in March 1944, St Pancras Services were sent to support Fulham and Hammersmith (see p 69).

16 Early in the war, the new Minister of Home Security, Herbert Morrison, changed the title from ARP to CD saying 'let us sweep away this jejune and unsuitable title', CD thereafter covered a much wider field of passive defence activities than ARP.

17 This, the heaviest raid to date, was known as 'the Thursday' and was followed two nights later, on 19/20 April, by another heavy raid known as 'the Saturday'. As a result of 'the Thursday' raid some 14,658 Londoners were admitted to LCC first-line Rest Centres – the largest number admitted in one day during the whole of the war. In St Pancras that Thursday night, ARP Warden C W Catlin was killed at Chalk Farm underground station and Warden W E Baptist was killed in Tottenham Court Road (see p 4).

18 On 10/11 May 1941, the last raid of the main Blitz on London, three St Pancras ARP Wardens (S Barnett, L East and F Thomson) died as a result of injuries suffered on duty in Mackworth Street NW1, while Stretcher Party Leader F A Grace died of injuries sustained that night in nearby Albert Street NW1 (see p 4).

Standing By

Notes for this chapter are on p 34

On the 23 June 1941 a cricket match was played at Lord's Cricket Ground – St Pancras v. Hampstead. Hampstead won the match. Our thanks are due to Sir Pelham Warner and the MCC for the use of the ground on this and subsequent occasions.

During August Councillor J D Wright, the Deputy Chief Warden, died. Cllr Wright was a popular members of the Council, and did good work on organising the Fire Guard in the early days. A Memorial Service was held at St Pancras Church, followed by a public funeral, at which the Wardens' Service was well represented.

Mr F O Woodburn Bamberger was appointed Deputy Chief Warden.

At the end of the month Dr J H Briscoe-Smith, ARP Medical Officer, resigned from the Council to take up a Government appointment abroad. He had done excellent work for the Stretcher Party Service and had the satisfaction of seeing the results of his labours put into practice during the Blitz.

During September Post Warden Rogers produced an apparatus to amplify faint sounds coming from a demolished building which proved satisfactory on its trials. Arrangements were made for a van to be ready to convey Mr Rogers and his

9 CD Personnel relaxing in ARP HQ canteen
Most of the ARP/CD workers were volunteers, who served their community having worked in their normal employment during the day. From 1943, an element of compulsion was introduced: volunteers could then only retire with official approval, and 'Fire Guard' duties (48 hours per month) were made compulsory. The young lady in khaki sitting on the right is probably a member of the Women's Legion, an organisation authorised by the War Office to wear uniform and seconded to St Pancras to drive the Control Car, Mobile Canteen and Utility Van. Five drivers, on 24-hour on-call shifts, were used.

apparatus to an incident when required [see also p 60].

On the 30th Mrs Winston Churchill visited the Borough and inspected the Depot at Old William Ellis School. She saw the workshop and the equipment for making toys which the men had got together, and expressed great interest in the toys made for children from timber taken from bombed premises.

In October Mr E T Milburn was appointed Staff Officer to the Medical Officer of Health, responsible for supervising and training Stretcher Party personnel. The ARP Committee also decided that 24 female paid staff should be engaged to run the Control Room and South Reporting Centre in place of male staff.

In November Councillor E A Minter was elected Mayor. The retiring mayor, Alderman Evan Evans, had done wonderful work for the people of St Pancras: the moment bombs dropped he was out and about in the Borough, doing all he could to help the unfortunate citizens who had been blitzed. Frequently he ignored official instructions and got things done quickly. He also attended the funerals of air raid victims, and liked to look personally into any case of real distress.

In January 1942 young members of the Civil Defence Force began to be called up for the Forces. This greatly reduced the number of parties available for Rescue work. On 21 March the North Report Centre, Pratt Street, was closed and the voluntary staff were transferred to duty at the Control Room, St Pancras Town Hall. This made a big difference to the hours of duty of all shifts, which had since early 1940 been doing duty from 6 p.m. to 9 a.m. every fourth night. The volunteers from North Report Centre made up two extra shifts, making a total of six shifts doing one night in six, including weekends, when the hours of duty were Saturday 1 p.m. to 9 a.m. next morning and on Sundays from 9 a.m. to 9 a.m. on Monday. All meals could be obtained at the Town Hall Canteen, paid for by subsistence money [9]. The six shifts were arranged as follows: No.1 Shift Mr G S E Barker, No.2 Mr A A Davey, No. 3 Mr W C W Roworth, who in his retirement was succeeded by Mr R C E Austin, No. 4 Mr C S Bainbridge, No. 5 Mr R Lee and No. 6 Mr P C Taylor.

The North Report Centre had done good work since the outbreak of war under the guidance of Mr W H Mathews, who also was of great assistance to Mr Roworth when he was Communications Officer.

For workers on site, a mobile canteen was presented to the Council through the generosity of an American donor, via the WVS [see p 65 for a picture of this canteen in operation]. A mobile library, for use by those unable to get to a library under wartime conditions, was provided by the Council [10, 11 on pp 30, 31].

At the beginning of March the Stretcher Party Service was reorganised, trained in Rescue duties and renamed the Light Rescue Service.[19] The St Pancras personnel attended the Heavy Rescue School, and the Heavy Rescue Officers at the Depots gave every assistance. The Light Rescue Leaders found the training very interesting and they could then carry out certain tasks of rescue work previously carried out by Heavy Rescue, reducing the waiting time until casualties had been removed by Heavy Rescue. The Light Rescue Parties in their turn gave First Aid instruction to members of the Heavy Rescue Service.

During August the Invasion Defence Scheme came into being; ARP Controller Mr C S Bainbridge was appointed Invasion Defence Officer, and Chief Warden and ARP Officer Councillor J E Davies MBE, Deputy Invasion Officer. The idea was to co-ordinate to full advantage all activities that would help in the event of an invasion. The support of local authorities, Ministries, Home Guard, Police, NFS and Public Utility companies would be placed at the disposal of the Invasion Defence Officer. Great care was taken in the choice of Reception Centres, Rest Centres, Evacuation Schemes and Billeting in order to avoid repetition of the French experience of a hysterical population fleeing from the enemy, assisted in their hysteria by well-placed Fifth Columnists.

A census was taken showing the number of people, the occupied and unoccupied houses, flats, stores, cars, vehicles, horses, in the Borough at the time. Excellent work was done by Food Control in arranging special dumps and stores to be earmarked to store essential supplies. Emergency rations were put together, the amount per person being:

Canned Beef	1½ lb per week
Flour	7 lb per week
Sugar	2 lb per week
Tea	2 oz per week
Margarine	12 oz per week
Milk	3 tins of condensed milk per person for fortnight

The flour was to be delivered to bakers; stores of fodder for horses were got together.

The Public Utilities Companies paid special attention to alternative means of supply or repairs in the case of disruption of gas, electric light or water. Arrangements were made for the homeless, for decontamination of gas-contaminated casualties. Food Inspectors trained special squads to deal with contaminated food. The Londoners' Meals Service[20] and Civil Defence Canteens were brought into the scheme; facilities for cooking in public places, streets etc. were established and in many places ovens were erected.

Retailers' and householders' supplies were increased so that they should all have three weeks' supply of food in hand. All LCC schools were to be notified in event of Invasion. The National Fire Service gave information about the petrol stocks they held which could be used, also a list

10 St Pancras Travelling Library (outside)
As people spent many nights in their bomb shelters, the St Pancras Library Service delivered books to the larger shelters. Many shelters had their own bookshelves.

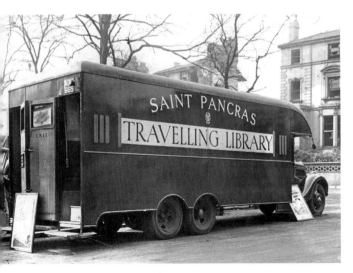

of buildings in the Borough which were considered to be 'High Fire Risk'. Lists were made of all the First Aid Posts available for walking wounded. Special stocks of coal were procured by the Borough and stored in special dumps. The LCC Rest Centres and Day Nurseries arranged to deal with homeless children. Information was to be disseminated to the public by police loudspeaker car. The manpower and labour question was to be dealt with by the respective Ministries. Should communications break down, police motorcyclists or cyclists were to be used. The Metropolitan Water Board supplied a list of wells that might be used in an emergency and also arranged for tank wagons to supply water. In the event of a breakdown of water supplies the Council arranged for 1200 chemical closets to be supplied. The General Post Office made arrangements and supplied a list of alternative post offices to be used should regular offices be put out of action. The Council and the London County Council made arrangements over any sewage problems that might arise.

The Scheme divided the Borough into four Districts, with a District Warden in charge of each District. The WVS appointed Women District Leaders, the Billeting Officers appointed four ladies and the Citizens Advice Bureau did likewise.

Essential features of this Scheme were the maintenance of essential services, distribution of food, conserving of water and fuel, rendering assistance to Public Utility Companies, provision of emergency sanitation, cooking and burial. "The provision for cooking, sanitation, refuse collection and burial squads in each post is definitely indicated." A Sanitary Inspector was appointed to each District. The Officer commanding the Air Training Corps arranged that 70 Cadets should be posted to each of the four Districts and a further 70 to the Town Hall, to act as messengers. The organisation of this Scheme reflects great credit on the Invasion Defence Officer and his Department, especially in view of their many other duties.

No more raids took place in St Pancras until October 1943. Services had to be reorganised because of the many call-ups. Rescue Parties (Heavy and Light) were well occupied in clearing the sites damaged during the April and May raids.

Early in 1943 a number of police officers, wardens and other members were trained as Qualified Bomb Reconnaissance Officials. District Wardens Riggs, Blane and Avery, Chief Instructor Bettles and Instructors Barnard and Slocombe attended a course arranged by the Home Office dealing with all types of bombs, including anti-personnel bombs, the recognition of an unexploded bomb (which frequently exploded later underground) and full details of precautions to be taken when a UXB is suspected. The members from Civil Defence were called Qualified Reconnaissance Officials Civil Defence (QRCD). Each official was given a proficiency certificate in bomb reconnaissance issued by the Chief Bomb Disposal Officer, London. To ensure that qualified personnel were kept in touch with the latest developments the certificates were renewed every six months. The Group Bomb disposal officer met each QRCD in his area every 2-3 months and got to know each one personally. Control Room duties were shared with the QRP (Police). One night when a large number of explosive incendiary bombs were dropped, 33 suspected UXBs were reported, every one of which was verified. All had to be inspected, a report given on each one and a certificate forwarded to London Region giving full particulars of the suspected UXB, and the basis of verification.

During July an Invasion Defence Scheme for dealing with Commando raids was received. It stated that the ringing of church bells would no longer be used as a warning of invasion or Commando raids and that no alternative audible signal would be used. All CD personnel should know how to recognise enemy parachute troops. Neither airmen bailing out of damaged aircraft nor parachute mines should be reported as parachute troops. Enemy parachute troops could easily be recognised as follows:-

They will not be more than 500 feet up. They will only be in the air for 10-30 seconds.

There will be 6-20 parachutes seen not more than 200 yards apart.

"It will be necessary to prepare plans for the calling out of the Home Guard.

Invasion Defence Officers are asked to concert plans in consultation with the Home Guard, police, WVS etc. These arrangements are based on the assumption that a raid will come between dusk and dawn."

A Military Liaison Officer was appointed who attended many exercises in the Control Room; special arrangements had to be made for co-operation between the Military, the Controller on the Civil Defence side, and the requirements of the Invasion Defence Officer, all using the same map and telephones – a pretty picture, causing many headaches and a lot of sorting out.

During May the Administrative Centre was opened at King's Cross Coaching Station. The WVS were already installed upstairs and were now joined by the Billeting and Rehousing Department under Mr W J Dale, the Citizens Advice Bureau and a Salvage Office for removal and storage of furniture enquiries. The Main Hall was turned into a general enquiry bureau, where, immediately after a raid, representatives of the Assistance Board, Food Office, and National Registration Officials opened their respective sections and continued until all ordinary enquiries

11 St Pancras Travelling Library (inside, with CD personnel) Particularly after the end of the main blitz in May 1941, the long hours of duty served by the ARP/CD Services were relieved by the regular provision of library books by the visiting St Pancras Library Service.

had been settled. The WVS gave splendid assistance in manning the General Enquiry Bureau, taking full particulars from all enquirers and entering them on a record card that was taken to the various departments, which saved the unfortunate people from saying the same thing over and over again.

The following month the procedure for dealing with 'crash raiding' came into being. Crash raiding was a mass attack on one town, on one objective. The procedure applied to the whole of the London Region, the Target being the ground that lies within 2 miles' radius of the focal point of the attack. London Region would determine the focal point and therefore the target area; the rest of London Region was considered to be outside this area and therefore able to release the majority of their Services to assist.

All Boroughs formed 'Area Control Points', which were a combination of Depot and Report Centre. At these points would be grouped Heavy and Light Rescue Parties [12], ambulances and cars,

12 Light and Heavy Rescue Squads at the Old William Ellis School, Allcroft Road NW5 The Heavy Rescue Service was the responsibility of the London County Council, the Light Rescue teams (previously, Stretcher Parties) that of St Pancras Council. Operationally, both were controlled by the Borough ARP Controller.

Mobile Medical Units, some Wardens and Messengers.

The Area Control Officers would take over from the Depot Superintendent the operational control of the Depot. The Borough was divided into four Area Controls with a District Warden in charge of each Depot as Area Control Officer. If the Borough was outside the target area, we were likely to be called upon for reinforcements of all Services. It was arranged that when telecommunication with the Control Room failed, Wardens Posts would report to the relevant Area Control.

Incident Control Points, by contrast, were set up for a short time near an incident requiring coordination of several services [13].

One of the most interesting incidents occurred at Birkenhead Street on 18 October 1943, the first big incident in St Pancras since the end of the 'Blitz' in May 1941. The lessons learned from the 'Blitz' and the reorganisation of the Services came into use for the first time. The bomb fell in the street, striking the end of a public surface shelter (which stood up to the shock very well and although it was occupied, none of the occupants was killed), demolishing three houses and doing heavy blast damage on both sides of the road. This end of Birkenhead Street had been badly damaged in 1940, and fortunately the houses on the west side

were unoccupied. The casualties were 11 killed, 21 seriously injured and taken to hospital and 40 with minor injuries. The Services were quickly on the spot, the former Stretcher Parties making their first appearance as Light Rescue Parties – and very good work they did. Control was able to call up the Group Mobile Squad, which included cranes, skips etc. which made it possible to move the debris from the site in two lorries and remove it; this made rescue work much quicker and all casualties were cleared in 62 hours, a remarkable achievement – an experience which proved its value when the V1 attacks started 9 months later. Besides the houses demolished, 17 more had to be pulled down, 14 more were made uninhabitable and 50 received minor damage.

The WVS opened an Enquiry point, the first one in London, and gave great assistance to the Salvage Officer in sorting and listing personal property recovered from the debris. The Administrative centre proved of great value, especially as it was so close to the incident.

This month also saw the first use of the Butterfly Anti-Personnel Bomb, quite a small thing, about the size of a packet of 50 cigarettes. These anti-personnel bombs had three types of fuses, and seldom exploded on impact; the main danger was that if one exploded, it exploded a number more, over a considerable area. Special search parties had to be trained and instructions were issued to the public. Fortunately none fell in St Pancras. It is difficult to understand why they were not used more, as they would have proved a serious menace and a great handicap to the movement of the Services.

In November Deputy Controller Mr W C W Roworth retired from the Council's Service. He had been very keen on Civil Defence from the start, and was mainly responsible for the training and efficiency of the Control Room. The Town Clerk, Mr R C E Austin, became Deputy Controller.

The beginning of 1944 saw the passing of Dr Maitland-Radford, the Medical Officer of Health. Dr Radford took a very active part in ARP from the beginning, worked

13 Leaders of Service Parties reporting to Incident Control Point
Representatives of the Mobile Medical Unit, Wardens and Rescue Squad reporting to the Incident Officer, who wore the letters IO on his sleeve.

hard during the Munich Crisis and at all times took an active interest in the medical services; he was greatly liked by all and sadly missed.

In February a most unusual incident occurred in Grafton Road. A complete container of incendiary bombs struck a house and exploded, the house was burned out in a few minutes. The National Fire Service prevented the fire from spreading, but 5 people were killed and everything in the house was completely destroyed. A large number of gas meters in adjacent houses urgently needed attention.

During March 1944 a number of incendiary bombs were dropped in the Borough. Severe damage was done to the top floors of Windsor House, damage was also done in Oakley Square and other districts. A number of incendiary bomb fires were never reported, the householders dealing with the fires themselves; the following day a personal call had to be made at each house in the affected area to ascertain what damage had been done. The Salvage Department collected a large quantity of bedding and blankets which had to be dried before the owners could use them.

During April, lectures were given to all Services on Security, pointing out the importance of 'Careless Talk'; at the same time a secret circular was issued that pilotless aircraft and some form of Long Range Rockets might be used in the near future. Arrangements were made to reinforce and support the London boroughs with military reinforcements which included infantry, Royal Engineers, Pioneers, Military Ambulances, Home Guard, and Mobile Columns of CD from other Regions. Elaborate arrangements were made, but fortunately the need for them never materialised. The Controllers of each Borough had attended a secret conference at Regional Headquarters in December 1943, when the new form of attack was discussed. Another circular was issued about this time regarding the use of a smoke screen over London. A tale is told, from a reliable source (like all tales), that one night it worked so well and was so dense that no buses or trams could move, thereby holding up all the traffic.

The merry month of May produced a circular that should live for ever as a perfect example of Regional Control and red tape. This circular was marked 'Security' and contained instructions from the Regional Commissioners re. revised marking on official documents, namely Top Secret, Secret, Confidential and Restricted. "TOP SECRET documents must be sent in double envelopes, the inner one addressed 'Top Secret' to be opened personally by ____ followed by the name, designation and address of the person and MUST be sealed down with wax. The outer envelope must NOT be marked as above, but must be marked Personal. These envelopes must only be opened by the addressee or his personal representative. They must be handled only by the person specifically designated and must not be disclosed to any other person. They must be kept under lock and key. They must never be sent by post, a despatch rider or messenger must be used. The receipt of 'Top Secret' documents must be acknowledged at once; documents that have so far been issued as 'Most secret' should now be regarded as 'Top Secret'."

Pages more followed, but the fact remains that at all times any secret documents handed to the Controller were in very safe hands, who out-Baldwined Baldwin for 'sealed lips'.

Notes

19 This was just one of the many measures taken to save and make better use of the limited manpower available to the Civil Defence Services. Later, some Home Guard and National Fire Service members were also trained in rescue work to assist the hard-worked Rescue Parties by the time of the V weapon offensives.

20 Londoners' Meals Service, like the Schools Meals Service and Civic Restaurants, were LCC responsibilities.

Flying Bombs
('Fly Bombs') and Rockets

Notes for this chapter are on p 37

June 1944 saw a new form of attack on London, something quite different from the normal raid. Six months previously we had been warned to expect some form of attack from pilotless aircraft.

The Control Room staff had been trained to receive the message PAC – Pilotless Air Craft, but just when everybody had got used to it the name was changed to FLY BOMB. The warning was sounded as usual, a few minutes later a strange terrifying noise would be heard, then a great black monster would come rushing across the sky, leaving a trail of flame behind it. Londoners soon got used to this beast, commonly called 'that doodle bug', learned its habits, soon found out that if the engine was still running when it passed over, your district was safe, but when the engine cut out and the 'doodle' started to glide silently along, then one had to dash for cover, because at the end of the glide, which sometimes was brief, the 'Fly-bomb' would suddenly hurtle to the ground. A few seconds later up came the smoke and then the explosion, many casualties and hundreds of homes damaged. The Civil Defence would be on their way carrying out their rescue work a few minutes later. The fly bombs dropped on St Pancras can be conveniently split into two groups, rather than a series of incidents, all very much alike, which would be very monotonous. We in St Pancras should be grateful for our open spaces, for half the number of fly bombs dropped in the Borough fell in open spaces, on railway property or on old bomb sites, doing little damage and few casualties.

The Long Range Rocket was a different proposition: no warning was given, nothing was seen or heard approaching; bang, the damage was done, very similar to fly-bomb damage[21], but in some cases, a little heavier[22]. It is a strange fact that if you were a mile away, the explosion appeared louder than if you were just outside the danger area.

The Tottenham Court Road district, the destination of most other types of enemy bombs, had its share of these new missiles, fly-bombs falling in Whitfield Street between Windmill Street and Goodge Street and at the corner of Howland Street and Tottenham Court Road, both dropping within a few days of each other and both at mid-day. The Whitfield 'doodle' demolished a number of homes and caused heavy blast damage in Goodge Street, Windmill Street and Colville Place.[23] Post Warden King and some of his Wardens were trapped in Wardens' Post 37, but fortunately managed to get out unhurt and were able to carry on their duties. A number of the houses damaged were occupied by foreigners living under very crowded conditions, indeed in one house an incredible number of people lived, sometimes sleeping three in a bed, most of them unable to speak English, making things very difficult for the CD Services. As the incident happened during the day, rescue work could proceed smoothly, but the damaged property was very old, making conditions difficult for rescue work. In one shop a lot of money and cigarettes were recovered, all of which were carefully checked by the owners, without a word of thanks to those who had risked their lives to recover the goods. The many restaurants in Charlotte Street escaped serious damage even though it was their busiest time. The Howland Street incident was more serious, the doodle demolishing a café, wrecking two motor buses, badly damaging a public house, a bank, many shops and workshops, and making a number of homes in Howland Street uninhabitable. Help from University College Hospital [14, p 36] was quickly on a scene that was indescribable – dead and injured all over the place, as well as the two buses, now only skeleton vehicles; a motor vehicle was blown off the road into the basements of some houses demolished after the Blitz in 1941. The total number of casualties for the two incidents amounted to 82 dead, 196 seriously injured, and 379 slightly injured.

The WVS opened Incident Inquiry Points and were kept fully occupied for many days. The Salvage department had two new problems to solve. First, the owner of a dyers & cleaners that was badly damaged was in the Forces and his mother, who carried on the business for him, was injured in the shop. As a result a huge number of people called at the Salvage Office to claim their goods. Second, a working tailor's shop was badly damaged, and all the contents were missing. Many West End tailors arrived, claiming uniforms and suits that were urgently required. In fact one officer could not return to his unit without his new tunic. These problems were all sorted out, most of the goods were recovered, and many harassed people were satisfied. At a later date a Long Range Rocket fell on Whitefield's Tabernacle, Tottenham Court Road, located between the two previous incidents.[24] This happened late at night, when very few people were about, the casualties were small and the damage to property was moderate.

Two hospitals were damaged by fly bombs. The West End Hospital for Nervous Diseases[25] in the Outer Circle, Regent's Park, standing in its own grounds, received a direct hit. Half the hospital was demolished, with 12 dead and 22 seriously injured. A second bomb fell on the Royal Free Hospital in Gray's Inn Road, striking an unoccupied block of buildings. This was an eerie experience for those in the street, as no damage was apparent from the outside, and no knowledge of what had happened inside, except for a long procession of ambulances coming

and going. Green Line coaches[26] were immediately commandeered by Control and were standing by when called for. The hospital was evacuated in a very short time; 5 people were killed and 67 seriously injured. Officials from London Region arrived to inspect the damage and were pleased to find what excellent work had already been done.

Four fly bombs fell in a line on different dates across the centre of the Borough. The first to fall in St Pancras fell in the early hours of the morning in Clarence Way at the corner of Torbay Street, demolishing the four corner houses and badly damaging a great many more. The services arrived quickly on the spot, bringing with them flood-lighting sets, which as it was the first occasion they had been used caused a little argument with the police, but they proved of the greatest value to the Rescue Service. A number of members of the Home Guard turned out, keeping the crowd back and guarding shops that had been damaged in Kentish Town Road. The Salvage department experienced great difficulty in dealing with this incident as the staff had been cut to a minimum. Assistance was given in loading vehicles by the National Fire Service, Light Rescue Service and Highways Department. The available storage accommodation was soon filled and additional storage found.

The second bomb fell in Rochester Place, a mews north of St Pancras Way. A whole block of the houses in St Pancras Way had to be demolished. The next fell in Hawley Road, causing a large crater and doing serious damage to a surface shelter in which a number of people were killed.

14 Ambulance arriving at University College Hospital (Grafton Way)

Rumours circulated that the shelter was not soundly constructed, but officials from the Ministry of Home Security found that the shelter conformed to the standard laid down. Another unfortunate happening at this incident was that a number of people who had been re-housed from Clarence Way and Torbay Street were again rendered homeless, also a number of houses were damaged for the second time.

The fourth fly bomb fell on a factory in St Pancras Way during the early afternoon. The Roof Watcher saw it coming, gave the local warning, workers quickly took cover in the firm's shelters, the result being that only ten people were killed – a splendid example of factory discipline and proof of the value of a factory alarm system.[27]

The casualties at these four incidents amounted to 42 killed, 68 seriously injured and 177 with minor injuries. The damage to house property was a serious problem. The first-aid repair organisation was tried to the utmost. The re-housing officer had a tremendous job to do to clear the Rest Centres. The Salvage Department was then working at seven different incidents.

A fly bomb fell in front of 57 Dartmouth Park Hill, facing the reservoir, doing a lot of damage, and it was indeed fortunate that houses were on only one side of the road. Another fell in Grafton Road by Warden Road, doing serious damage to houses and shops. Fly bombs also fell in Crowndale Road and Stanhope Street, but in each case the 'doodle' fell on an old bomb site. Another fell on railway property in Ossulston Street. The total casualties at these three incidents amounted to 1 killed, 21 seriously injured, and 67 minor injuries. Two fell in Regent's Park, and three in Parliament Hill Fields, causing no casualties and very little blast damage. Another fell in Waterlow Park,

causing considerable damage in Bisham Gardens and Highgate Cemetery. A Long Range Rocket fell in Tavistock Place, causing heavy casualties and damage to property in a Church Hall where a Congress was in progress. A number of clergymen were killed.[28] A member of the Control Room Staff had just left the Town Hall and was able to run back to the Control Room and order out the parties, thereby saving a lot of time in calling the Rescue Services as only one Wardens' Post in three was open during the hours of daylight.

All these incidents occurred at different times, which made them easier to handle, and much support was received from Group 1 in the form of Group Mobile Squads, cranes, lorries to remove the debris and Army searchlights. Also on one or two occasions, specially trained dogs were used to locate trapped people, all of which combined to make the rescue of casualties much quicker than was thought possible during the 1940/41 period. All services worked together well.

The Heads of Services can be truly proud of their labours; they will undoubtedly look back in days to come and wonder how the devil it was all accomplished. All had their moans and groans about this and that, but the fact remains that the system worked, and worked well. Credit should go to the planners at the top who laid down the law and saw it carried out. Those who were retained in the fourth line of defence, the Civil Defence Service, will always remember the work carried out under dangerous conditions and can safely say to themselves "I did my bit in the war and, thank God, was able to help numerous people who were passing through an awful crisis in their lives."

---

21 Both the V1 and V2 carried a 1-ton HE warhead.
22 Across Britain, just over two people were killed by each V1 but five by each V2 – so the losses in St Pancras from the two V1 incidents were by comparison heavy.
23 The small public garden with its bench seats at the junction of Colville Place and Whitfield Street was later established on the site of the Colville Place houses destroyed by this V1 Flying Bomb.
24 Rebuilt as the American Church on the Tottenham Court Road site.
25 Just inside Regent's Park, near Gloucester Gate.

The site has not again been built on.
26 Green Line coaches were used as auxiliary ambulances and as hospital transport from the time of the 1938 Munich crisis.
27 The Roof Spotter system enabled the factory and its workers to continue working until a weapon was judged to be a direct threat when staff could rapidly take refuge in their air raid shelter.
28 This was the Regent Square V2 incident (Judd St incident) of 9 February 1945 when 7 members of the HQ staff of the Presbyterian Church of England were killed; several more people were killed as they walked past the Hall.

Winding Up

I n 1945 two Long Range Rockets dropped in St Pancras, but the advance of the Allied Armies through Belgium and Holland into Germany prevented further damage to the country as the rocket sites were captured.[29] On 26 April the Ministry of Home Security issued a circular which stated "When the Government decide that the Civil Defence Organisation is no longer needed for the purposes of the War, steps will be taken to wind up the war organisation of the Civil Defence General Services. The date decided on for the initiation of this action will be notified to local authorities in due time, and will be termed the Appointed Day." Six days later the appointed day was named: 2 May 1945. All CD Services were given one month's preliminary notice, followed by one month's final notice. Persons desiring to be released could do so on giving one month's notice, whole and part-time members were allowed to retain their battle dress, greatcoats, steel helmets, respirators, eye shields and anti-gas ointment. VE Day was celebrated on the 8th and 9th of May, both days being a general holiday. A third VE Day was granted later.

Control Room Voluntary Duty ceased on 2 May. Fifty-six members of the Council's staff had continued their rota of duty from 31 August 1939 to 2 May 1945, duties varying from the commencement from every other night to one night in three, and finally one night in six. On Sunday 13 May the Mayor and Councillors attended a special service of Thanksgiving at St Pancras Church, Euston Road. A large contingent of the CD Services marched to the church from Camden Town, led by the Controller, Mr C S Bainbridge, the Heads of Services marching with their detachments. The WVS, the Home Guard and other organisations were represented. The church was very full and the service, conducted by the Vicar assisted by the CD Choir, was much appreciated and enjoyed by all present. After the service the Mayor, Alderman J H Mitchell, entertained the Councillors, Chief Officers of the Council and Heads of Services, at the Town Hall. During the next few weeks, people started to return to civil life, and many familiar faces disappeared. The Town Hall looked different, the blackout disappearing from the windows, which gave a surprising appearance after so many years. Letters of thanks were sent to all ranks on p 40.

A special invitation was sent by the Mayor to the St Pancras Civil Defence Services to attend a Farewell Parade at the Zoological Gardens, Regent's Park, on Saturday 9 June 1945. All Services were asked to attend, but the numbers were disappointing as so many had already left the Services. A good muster from the Wardens' Service, however, made the Parade an impressive one. Councillor J E Davies MBE, Chief Warden and ARP Officer, was in charge of the Parade. A band was provided by the ATC [Air Training Corps] Cadets. The parade was inspected by the Mayor, who was introduced to the Chief Officers by the Controller. After the inspection the ARP Controller, Mr C S Bainbridge, addressed the parade and gave an excellent appreciation of the services rendered by all ranks and expressed his personal thanks and pride in their achievement. The Mayor also thanked those in the parade, on behalf of the Borough, for their wonderful work, and formally dismissed the CD Services by giving a very good word of command. After the parade, the Members of Council, Chief Officers and Heads of Services were entertained to tea by the Mayor. All services attending the parade had admission to the Zoo and a ticket for refreshments. This was the official end of Civil Defence. No written account can do justice to the work done, the difficulties encountered, or the wonderful spirit of the people.

A good example of the Cockney spirit was the old lady who lived in the King's Cross area. Her house was badly damaged, and when told that she would have to move out at once and asked what she would like done with her chattels, had she got an address or would she like her chattels taken to the Council's Stores, the old lady burst into tears and said, 'Oh sir, you are so kind to me.' Real gratitude for assistance, and a kind word, and no thought of her own troubles.

On 30 June 1945 Mr Bainbridge resigned his position as ARP Controller, and for the first time since the summer of 1938 was able to devote his full time to the work of Borough Engineer and Surveyor. The position of ARP Controller was one that required great tact and keen understanding. The Controller had to smooth out the troubles of the different services, be responsible to the ARP Committee for all matters appertaining to Civil Defence, including shelter accommodation, negotiating with London Region or Group on various matters, mastering the contents of hundreds of circulars, taking the responsibility for the handling of incidents, receiving deputations from disgruntled citizens – in other words 'carrying the baby' for all things – a thankless, never-ending job, well carried out, a job which was fully appreciated by the Council and marked by a special vote of thanks in Council. On Mr Bainbridge's retirement,

Cllr Davies, Chief Warden and ARP Officer, took over the winding up of Civil Defence, a big job involving the checking and handing in to stores equipment and clothing of the various services, fire guard equipment, dismantling the Control Room and ARP Depots, the closing of Wardens' Posts, etc. Cllr Davies was Deputy Chief Warden at the outbreak of war and remained at ARP Headquarters until the end of September 1945, carrying a number of appointments. Throughout the war the ARP Committee continued meeting, most of the time once a week. Alderman Sir David Davies and Councillor F W Powe JP were members for the full period, Alderman J H Mitchell for most of the time. The Committee always had a large agenda to discuss, complicated circulars to understand, they interviewed hundreds of people and made a great number of appointments. The Controller was always present to give facts and figures, and when required, Heads of Departments also attended. The Mayor was Chairman of the Committee, as well as attending to the affairs of the Lord Mayor's Distress Fund, which meant interviewing hundreds of people each week. The ARP Committee carried out their duties with distinction for the Borough, and it is hoped with satisfaction to themselves.

29 The last V2 rocket to hit London was on the morning of 27 March 1945, falling on the Hughes Mansions flats in Stepney.

To the Members of the Saint Pancras Civil Defence (General) Services

Now that the time has come for the Civil Defence (General) Services to be demobilised, I feel that I can safely relinquish the office of A.R.P. Controller, which I propose to do at the end of June. None could say in 1939 what our experience of air raid attack would mean to us, our people and our homes, but now that we are at the end of the journey, we can say that the Civil Defence Services .have completed a first class job of work.

I am proud of the Saint Pancras Civil Defence Organisation and would like to express my deep appreciation and warm thanks to each of you for your help and co-operation. The success achieved has been the result of all appreciating the value of team spirit, self sacrifice and good fellowship.

On Saturday, 9th June, it is hoped to hold a farewell gathering, at which His Worship The Mayor will express his appreciation on behalf of the Borough Council, to the services, I hope that there will be a record attendance. To each of you I say Good Luck and God Speed.

C. S. BAINBRIDGE,
A.R.P. CONTROLLER

On the cessation of European hostilities, I wish to place on record my deep appreciation of the devoted manner in which all of the services connected with air raid precautions in the Borough had so nobly worked.

As you know, the Borough has suffered severely by enemy attacks and the duties you have all so splendidly discharged at all times of the day and night have been of the most exacting and onerous character. Never once has there been the slightest criticism of the magnificent manner in which you have undertaken the many tasks — often of an unpleasant nature - which have fallen to your lot, and as mayor, I must express on behalf of the Borough, my great admiration. Many grateful expressions of thanks have been received from the unfortunate sufferers you have been able to assist. To those of the services whose duties have not brought them directly into contact with the many disastrous raids we have suffered, but who have nevertheless assisted in the many necessary and arduous tasks, my thanks must also be extended. Every section of the services have rendered their best service with enthusiasm and cheerfulness. This fact has assisted tremendously in relieving the many sad problems.

The Government have expressed their view that the Local Authorities and their officers have co-operated with them whole-heartedly and that local government has fully justified the confidence that has been placed in it.

Although your duties have now come to and end, there is little doubt that the country will have need of your spirit, comradeship and service in the difficult days ahead.

To the voluntary workers — that numerous and painstaking body — I realise how much of your leisure time you have so freely devoted to the great cause you have served.

All of you should take many memories which you have a right to be proud, and to each one of you I offer my personal thanks for the unsparing manner in which you have tackled your great tasks.

J H MITCHELL,
MAYOR

Part II

Service Reports

by or with the advice of Heads of Services

The ARP
Special Emergency Committee

At the Council meeting held on 3 May 1939, the following Resolution was approved:

That the Council do appoint an Air Raid Precautions Emergency Committee consisting of three Members of the Council to act in co-operation with the A.R.P. Controller.

The first meeting of this Committee was held on Monday 4 September 1939, the day after war was declared. The Mayor (Councillor G A Watts JP), Alderman Sir David Davies JP (Metropolitan Water Board) and Councillor F W Powe JP (London County Council) formed the Committee. The Mayor was elected Chairman of the Committee each year. Alderman Sir David Davies and Councillor F W Powe served on the Committee up to the last meeting in October 1945.

In May 1940 the Committee was enlarged with the addition of two members. Alderman J H Mitchell served on the Committee until its last meeting, and Councillors Mrs C Haldane, C T E Fletcher, Mrs W Paul and J W K Maile also served on the Committee at various times. The work carried out by the Committee is difficult to appreciate, as the matters to be discussed and the decisions that had to be taken covered such a large range of items, from the appointment of ARP officials to the Borough Shelter programme. Each of the many items on the Agenda had to receive separate study, which in many instances necessitated reading long technical reports. The appointment of Depot Superintendents, senior Control Room Staff, Stretcher Party Shift Leaders or Supervisors and Fire Guard officials and many other services all had to have careful consideration. Rates of pay for the various appointments had to be fixed, and Home Security and London Regional Circulars required close study. The Borough Shelter Programme covered a vast range of various types of shelter to be erected.

Numerous official visits were made to the Borough. The Regional Commissioners, Sir Ernest Gowers and Admiral Sir Edward Evans[1], frequently visited to inspect different CD activities, with the ARP Committee always in attendance. Individual members of the Committee paid visits to ARP Depots, Shelters etc.

In all this work they had the advice and experience of the Controller, Mr C S Bainbridge, who was expected to have the latest information on all matters, in which he was assisted by the Deputy Controller, Mr W C W Roworth, and later by Mr R C E Austin. The Chief Warden and ARP Officer Councillor J E Davies MBE assisted in all matters relating to the Wardens' service, ARP Depots and the Fire Guard Organisation.

1 The regional system of government was introduced in London at the time of the Munich crisis with Sir John Anderson as the Commissioner – he having planned the system to keep the country going during a general strike whilst the Permanent Secretary at the Home Office in the 1920s. Anderson was brought into the government as a result of the crisis, as Lord Privy Seal, the minister responsible for National Service and Civil Defence. Sir Ernest Gowers (of *Complete Plain Words* fame) became London Senior Regional Commissioner in January 1941, dealing with the administration of the region, and Admiral Evans (Captain Scott's second in command and during World War I, '*Evans of the Broke*') was the 'outdoor' Commissioner, boosting morale by nightly visiting shelters and ARP workers under fire. See Robin Woolven 'The London Experience of Regional Government 1938-1945' *The London Journal* Vol. 20 No.2 (2000).

Members of The ARP Committee, 1939-1945

	The Mayor (Chairman)	The Committee
4/9/39	Cllr G A Watts JP	Ald. Sir David Davies JP, Cllr F W Powe JP
10/11/39	Ald. Evan Evans JP	Davies, Powe
3/5/40	Ald. Evan Evans JP	Davies, Powe, Ald. J W Mitchell, Cllr Mrs C Haldane
3/1/41	Cllr E A Minter	Davies, Powe, Mitchell, Cllr C T E Fletcher
7/3/44	Cllr E A Minter	Davies, Powe, Mitchell, Cllr Mrs C Haldane
10/11/44	Ald. J H Mitchell JP	Davies, Powe, Cllr J W Kingsley Maile, Cllr Mrs W Paul

Control Room

C S Bainbridge (Borough Engineer and Surveyor), Controller

One day in 1939, Mr W C W Roworth was asked to take over the Control Room. He had to think "What is a Control Room?" We heard that Control Room Procedures would be demonstrated at the Home Office ARP School, South Kensington, and Mr Roworth was allowed to watch the proceedings, which seemed to consist of a number of people walking round a table, each carrying a label stating who he represented. Fortunately he met a friend there who invited him to inspect a Control Room already in being. Mr Roworth and Mr Mathews at Pratt Street then got the Control Room and Report Centres going, and maintained the keenest interest in everyone involved, Mr Roworth until his retirement and Mr Mathews until the last night on duty. The Control Room was to be manned by voluntary shifts from the Authority's staff.

The London Region, covering an area of over 720 square miles, containing 6½ million people, was divided into 9 groups, each under the direction of a Group Coordinating Officer. St Pancras was one of the Boroughs in Group 2 (with Headquarters in the North West Polytechnic, Prince of Wales Road) together with Marylebone, Paddington, Hampstead, Stoke Newington and Islington. The main function of the Group was to provide mutual assistance within the Group; if the required assistance was not available within the group, reinforcements would be requested through London Region from an adjoining Group. St Pancras was divided into 37 Wardens' Posts, half the posts reporting to the North Report Centre, Pratt Street, the others to the South Report Centre at the Town Hall (see p 10).

When an incident occurred, the wardens would telephone an Express Report to the Report Centre [15, p 44], stating where the incident had taken place and whether there were casualties.

The procedure thereafter was changed several times, but the principle remained constant: the 'IN' telephonist would write down the message in quintuplicate, and the copies were passed to the Message Room Supervisor for logging by the Log Clerk; the Officer in charge of the Report Centre, who decided the number of parties to be despatched to the incident; the Resources Officer; and the Message Room, where the 'OUT' telephonists would ring a depot and Ambulance Station (e.g.[16], p 45) ordering out the necessary parties. The various copies of the Express Report showing what action the O.C. Report Centre had taken would then be passed round the Control Room, one copy going to the Controller or Sub-Controller on duty, one copy to the Medical Officer of Health or his deputy to be shared with the Heavy Rescue Officer, one copy to the Plotting Officer who would plot the incident on the Control Map and one copy to the Liaison Officer who would send the information to Group.

Further messages from the same incident would receive the original occurrence number for decisions to be taken as to whether further help should be despatched.

North Depot Centre was closed in March 1942, and all 37 Wardens' Posts then reported to the South Depot Centre. This caused a lot of anxiety, but as it turned out, we had no more mass raiding and the South depot was able to deal with all requirements.

The Sub-Controller was generally responsible for all actions to be taken at each air raid incident during his 24-hour tour of duty from 9 a.m. to 9 a.m. the following morning. He was also responsible that sufficient parties were sent to all incidents, that the police and Public Utility Companies were informed of relevant air raid damage, that all road blocks were reported to Group HQ, ARP Depots and Ambulance Stations, that the Liaison

15 Message Room, Report Centre

The complex efficient handling of messages into and out of the Town Hall Report Centre is detailed above.

Officer sent proper damage and situation reports to Group, to make certain that all homeless people were accommodated at rest centres, and when convenient visit the various sites, interview the Incident Officer and ensure that all possible assistance had been given to those who had lost their homes.

For the first two years the Control Room had a full-time staff of 9 men on duty on alternate nights. The voluntary shifts were nominally on duty from 9 a.m. to 9 a.m. the following day, but actually they carried out normal office duties during the day unless a day raid took place, when the shift on duty reported to the Control Room. The normal day-time duty was performed by a male supervisor and 3 women. The voluntary staff manned the 'Out' telephones in the Message Room and performed all the important tasks in the Control Room.

My memory of activity at the Control Room ([3], p 14) during a busy evening is something like this. The shift would come on at 5 p.m., have tea in the canteen, read the evening paper, then depart to various parts of the Town Hall basement. Some would play table-tennis, billiards or snooker, some played cards and some would talk to the girls. When the warning went from the siren at King's Cross, which sounded very loud in the basement, all play would stop and there was a general rush for the Control Room. In the Message Room, you would find six 'In' telephones manned by the paid

staff, headphones on, message pads before them, pencils well sharpened. The voluntary staff would man the six 'Out' telephones. The police and fire phones were under the watchful eye of the message supervisor.

Near the door sat the Log Clerk, giving each incident an occurrence number. Near him was the O.C. Report Centre. In the middle of the Control Room was a large table covered with the Control Room map. At the head of the table sat the Controller's Clerk, on his left the Controller's representative, down the side of the table facing the resources board sat the MOH or his deputy, next came the MOH representative, then the Heavy Rescue Officer and his deputy and his assistant. At the bottom of the table sat the Control Room supervisor in charge of the paid staff and Group reinforcements, while nearby was the Liaison Officer, the Group telephonist and the Ambulance Officer. Round the table was the Plotting Officer and the Borough Engineer's representative who had to see that all the damage to all the highways was attended to during the raid, and during the day check up on all road damage etc. Also there were four service telephonists who would make special calls for the Controller or take or send messages to Group. If there was a lull, say nothing happened for an hour, cards would appear, some would fade away to the corridor outside the Control, sleep in the deck chairs or play cards, all within sound of the telephone bell.

Frequently in 1940/42, the 'alert' would be on until daybreak. A very weary and tired shift would take breakfast in the canteen at 8 a.m. and at 9 a.m. take their place at their office desk, carrying on their normal duties.

Two important posts in the Control Room were the Liaison and Resources Officers. The Liaison Officer had to keep Group informed of all incidents, giving further particulars from time to time and at 5 a.m. forwarding a long and detailed Situation Report of the true position in the Borough. The Resources Officer also had a complicated job, keeping a close watch on the movement of all parties, mark on the Tally Board all parties out of depots and what incident they had gone to, mark them back again when they returned to depot as well as keeping track of group reinforcement into the Borough, or our parties going out of it. The Plotting Officer had to have a sound knowledge of the geography of the Borough, to enable him to plot very quickly on the Control Room map any incident reported. All these Control Room Officers held important positions on the Council staff and had to keep themselves up to date in the latest Control Room procedure, which

16 Ambulance station in St Albans Road NW5
Ambulances, both the regular and emergency vehicles, were the responsibility of the London County Council, but all were operationally controlled by the Borough ARP Controller.

meant reading a number of circulars and attending many Control Room Exercises.

The Fly Bomb[2] procedure was different, because in nearly every case they came one at a time, sometimes with many days in between. When a fly bomb dropped in or near the Borough during office hours, the shift on duty reported immediately to the Control Room, half the Town Hall staff seemed to ring up the Control Room to find out where it had fallen, while the other half would rush to the windows or on to the roof to try and locate the smoke. Reports would come in from many people who thought they knew where it had dropped, and these had to be checked. Once the Rescue Parties had been ordered out, most of the voluntary shift were able to return to their normal duties. Some of the incidents kept the Control Staff busy for many days. After the first week of this new menace, a large number of Light and Heavy Rescue Parties ([12], p 32) and Ambulances were immediately despatched and were usually able to cope with the incident; as the bombs arrived as singletons, relief parties were always obtainable.

Week-end duty in the Control Room was always a trial. Reporting for duty at 9 a.m. on a bright sunny Sunday morning and remaining on duty until 9 a.m. on Monday morning was a great test of loyalty, especially if no incidents occurred, but it was conscientiously carried out by the staff. The Canteen was open for meals throughout the day, closing at 9 p.m., but tea and sugar were provided at 11.30 p.m. and more supplies were available in the Control Room for use should an incident occur in the early hours of the morning.

At Christmas time each shift had a Christmas Shift party and many bright ideas were produced, one shift putting on a pantomime.

For many years the Wardens' Service provided a 'guard' at the Town Hall, during office hours at the entrance to the Control Room and after office hours at the main entrance, where everybody entering the Town Hall was expected to produce a pass.

The Council officials who put in such a vast amount of voluntary work cannot be praised too highly. There was a good team spirit in every shift, and many after the war missed the comradeship of the Control Room

2 Known in later years as *flying bombs*; the nomenclature 'fly bombs' was used throughout the war and in Cllr Newbery's account in November 1945.

Air Raid Shelter provision

Councillor J E Davies MBE, Chief Warden and ARP Officer;
G Dale, Chief Engineering Assistant for the Shelter Programme

The complexity of the subject here makes it impossible to chronicle the facts in chronological order. At least ten types of shelter were eventually produced, each with several design phases and subsequent modifications.

The Air Raid Precautions Act of 1937 inaugurated Civil Defence, and from this 'seed' emanated the Anderson shelter, which was designed as a 'Duck Hole', i.e. a place in which to dive when a bomb fell and exploded. This principle guided all designs of shelter up to the beginning of the Blitz in September 1940, when constant night bombing necessitated long sojourns in shelters designed only for short occupation (30 minutes at most). There was a clear need to provide lighting, ventilation etc. Finally, actual bombing conditions revealed inherent weaknesses and standard of protection.

The eventual provision of all types of shelter in the Borough is shown in the Table, with the approximate total cost in capital expenditure and in maintenance. For various reasons the allocation of the costs between the various types is approximate.

Type of shelter	Number provided	Seating capacity	Approximate cost
Anderson	7,000	35,780	£51,597
Domestic basements and coal vaults	2,456	28,568	£34,186
Domestic surface	1,547	7,634	£19,747
Communal surface	303	12,572	£63,990
Tenement shelters	146	12,798	£48,530
Public basements	40	15,184	£38,695
Trench shelters	34	17,029	£128,021
Public surface	79	11,961	£60,423
Morrison	1,221	2,952	£1,239
Strengthening all surface shelters			£107,718
Maintenance, all shelters			£136,033
Totals	**12,826**	**144,468**	**£690,179**

Trenches

This type of shelter may be called the 'Father', whilst the Anderson may be called the 'Mother' of all shelters. The Munich crisis in September 1938 with its threat of war made it imperative that this sort of shelter should be provided quickly; at this stage trench shelters were merely elaborate 'dug-outs' constructed by all available men on every available open space.[3] The emergency over, a halt was called, the position was reviewed in the light of cool reasoning, and some were filled in. Selected sites were eventually developed as permanent constructions. The main difficulty with these shelters was the infiltration of sub-soil water, and despite trial of all sorts of ingenious ideas, none attained 100% efficiency. An asphalt canopy over the whole of the block greatly assisted matters, but an admirable crop of thistles grew each year and pushed their way through the asphalt.

Anderson Shelters

In January 1939 the design of this type of shelter was announced by the Government

and actual deliveries began by March. At first intended for the gardens of two-storeyed houses only, this was extended shortly before the outbreak of war to include houses with three floors above ground level, and eventually to four floors if sufficient distance from the house could be obtained. The shelter was designed for short occupation only and the technical difficulties in adaptation for all-night use were almost insurmountable; a satisfactory solution at reasonable cost was never found. The sub-soil in this borough is, as in most of London, mainly clay and natural sub-soil drainage is practically non-existent, hence the everlasting attempts to keep the water out of these shelters.

An amazing number of householders signed a form refusing to allow installation of an Anderson shelter (provision of domestic shelters was always optional, but they could not be removed after installation). In October and November 1940, when the staff was extremely busy and neither shelters nor labour for their installation were available in sufficient quantity, the 'refusers' naturally demanded immediate shelter provision. Many of these people were instrumental in obtaining the opening of Tube Stations for shelter purposes.

Domestic Basement Shelters

At the onset these were considered expensive since a whole basement room had to adapted whether the number of residents was sufficient to use the shelter to its fullest capacity or not, but what a boon they

3   At the time of Munich, the following open spaces in St Pancras were excavated to provide trench shelters at a rate of 1,200 people per acre. Parliament Hill shelter for 1,000 people, Electricity Station 2,000 people, Camden Square 2,000 people, Primrose Hill 2,000 people, Regent's Park 6,000 people, Oakley Square 1,000 people, Euston Square 600 people, Gordon Square 2,000 people, Tavistock Square 2,000 people, Brunswick Square 2,000 people and Mecklenburgh Square 2,000 people. These sites provided a total of 23,200 places although the Table shows only 17,019 trench shelter places.

were in the dark days of 1940/41 when beds could be placed in the room and a good night's rest, if not sleep, obtained. For each basement a plan had to be made, space selected, a scheme prepared and a contract let for the work. Because of expense, wherever possible arched coal vaults under the pavement were adapted as shelters – they were admirable except for being inclined to be damp. When air raids did actually start a number of householders had to frantically shift over a ton of coal, and members of the Heavy Rescue Parties made some pungent remarks when they found, on removing the Emergency exit cover to the vault adjoining the shelter to release shelterers who were trapped, that they were expected to turn themselves into coal heavers.

Domestic Surface Shelters

This type was provided where the back yard was insufficient for an Anderson and there was no basement. Based on a surface area of 3.75 square feet per person they were small, and very many were unable to take a full-length bunk. Enlargement was not always possible. With prolonged night bombing they fell into disuse and the residents went out to public shelters.

Tenement Shelters

The Government programme of free provision of shelter to persons below a certain income[4] included occupants of working-class blocks of flats and tenement buildings. Because of the design and layout of these buildings, each block of flats required special consideration. The most competent person to deal with this matter was the owner's architect, who should have an intimate knowledge of the building, was more likely to obtain assisted cooperation from the owner and yet produce a scheme which would receive the approval of the Council's Technical Officer. These architects were appointed as Consultants to the Council for the work and were controlled through a Technical Assistant.

4 Initially supplied free for those householders earning not more than £250 p.a.

Communal Surface Shelters

There remained residents who could not be offered shelter by one of the types described above. In cases where these persons could not be accommodated in public shelters within reasonable distance of their homes, brick surface shelters were constructed either in the streets outside or on vacant ground adjoining. This type of shelter was the last type of domestic shelter to be constructed, with the exception of the much later Morrison Shelter, and the last shelter in the Borough was completed only in the summer of 1942. Their construction was hampered by shortage of materials, as were the public Surface Shelters dealt with later. The last 60 were of a much improved design, in reinforced concrete. Shortage of timber and skilled building labour made it imperative for new, ingenious methods to be devised to gain speed on the work. Many residents remembered after the War the curious combinations of steel girders which lumbered about the streets – particularly the resident who telephoned the police to make them aware that some madmen were loose on Dartmouth Park Hill (the main cradling of the shuttering was being shifted from Chester Road, down Dartmouth Park Hill, with a 3-ton lorry in reverse behind it to act as a brake). Towards the end, shelters were being mass-produced at a rate of four per week, employing a labour force of only 26 men, mostly unskilled.

Morrison Shelters

In 1941 the upper income limit for free provision of shelter was extended from £250 p.a. to £350 p.a. This naturally created considerable new demand for shelters when building labour was getting scarce owing to the call-up of skilled operatives to the Forces and the considerable number who were already engaged on other priority work. The demand was met by providing Andersons where suitable, and a new type of shelter that was produced after actual experience of bombing conditions. This was the 'Morrison' or Indoor Table Shelter. This shelter was again limited in scope, being unsuitable for buildings of more than three storeys, and many ratepayers considered officials of the Council to be obstructive because, having set their heart on an Indoor Shelter, they were told that their premises were not suitable. These shelters continued to be available right up to the end of the war, and many were issued to suitable premises during the period of the Fly Bombs and Rockets, whether the premises had been previously provided with shelter or not.[5]

Public Basement Shelters

The crisis of 1938 saw Technical Assistants surveying all basements of properties on the main streets. The information was shelved after 'Munich', but with the threat of war in August 1939 a list was made of all basements suitable as shelters.[6] At 7 p.m. on 31 August it was decided to inform the public that these premises would be used as shelters. While office staff were trying to contact occupiers of the premises concerned, without much success, a staff of four billposters was collected by 9.30 p.m., the district was divided into four and each billposter set out about 10 p.m. complete with transport and bills (which had been printed in 1938) and accompanied by an official. The whole task was completed by 4 a.m. The telephone was much in use

5 In October 1943, a further 100,000 Morrison (indoor) shelters were ordered and the large number of Morrisons held in reserve across the country were moved to stores around London. In the first two months of 1944 some 29,000 Morrisons were distributed in the London Region.

6 During the 'Munich' census, a total of 144 basements adjoining main thoroughfares were identified in St Pancras, capable of accommodating 56,000 shelterers. Those basements selected were strengthened with timber beams at government expense. The Table on p 46 states that only 15,184 public basement shelter places were provided.

17 Interior of ARP Shelter, 91 Pancras Road This shelter was in one of the brick arches under the railway lines into St Pancras Station. The triple bunks in this picture could accommodate 89 shelterers. Note the emergency lights for use in the event of a power failure. This former coal store site, using an arch under the raised railway lines approaching St Pancras station, was redeveloped when the St Pancras platforms (particularly Platform 13) were extended as part of the Channel Tunnel project.

next morning, and sleepless Assistants had to exercise great tact and patience. However, the move was justified, as practically every one of these shelters was used on the following Sunday.

Basements formed the nucleus of the public basement shelters; some were rapidly strengthened and undesirable ones gradually discarded in the light of experience. Of approximately 80 signposted, only 40 were in use at the end of the war. These shelters were first provided with bunks in lieu of seating ([17], p 49) then with canteens, lavatories and wash-places with running water, and the larger ones were strengthened and divided into smaller compartments, as actual experience of bombing and technical research indicated. The largest basement shelters, when being used extensively as Dormitory Shelters in Spring 1941, developed as a social experiment with full community amenities: a smoking room [!], canteen, recreation room with stage, and a full-sized Medical Aid post with a special bay for nursing and expectant mothers as well as a children's playroom.

Public Surface Shelters

Experience before 1939 led to the belief that aerial attack on London would be carried out by daylight. Night bombing was unheard of. The development of public shelters was originally based, therefore, on the assumption that persons anywhere on the streets in daylight should be able to find shelter within a reasonable distance. The police counted the number of persons anywhere in the main roads of the metropolis during daylight and forwarded these figures to Local Authorities. The

18 Underground shelter in Tube (at Swiss Cottage, not in St Pancras). Once people who were dramatically in need of a good night's sleep were allowed to shelter in London Underground stations, the government provided three-tier bunks (bunking) and basic sanitary facilities. Refreshment facilities were often provided. At this station, then on the Bakerloo Line, the shelterers started their own magazine ('The Swiss Cottager') which ran to five issues – copies of all of which are in Camden Local Studies Library.

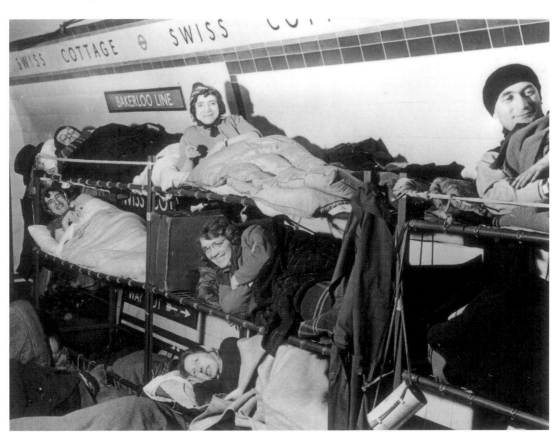

disposition of public shelters was planned after analysis of these counts. It was further decided that persons in main-line railway termini should be included (this Borough includes 3 of the 12 London termini). The trench and basement shelters obviously did not provide sufficient accommodation according to the police figures, and surface shelters had to be sited in the streets adjacent to, or on vacant sites near, the main roads. The scheme for these surface shelters had just got under way, as had the scheme for Communal Surface Shelters, when the retreat from Dunkirk [26 May to 3 June 1940] occurred. This created a demand for material for coastal defence which had to be met at the expense of the shelter programme. Bricks, steel and cement were very seriously affected. Happily, these shortages did not materially slow down the surface shelter programme. The brick shortage occurred first, and when it was realised that the brick company that was supplying the bricks could not keep up a sufficient daily rate of delivery (about 25,000), there followed a frantic two days of searching around

among other suppliers; 10 million bricks were required to complete the shelters, and on the second day two offers of 5 million bricks each at prices well over the original price allowance were made to an official over the telephone. Taking a deep breath, he took the plunge and clinched the deal, incurring an expenditure of £30,000, a procedure entirely foreign to Local Government practice.

No sooner was this position eased when Cement Control reared its head. Word was received on a Friday afternoon that this control would operate on the following Monday. Again frantic enquires were immediately made and every available piece of transport was ordered to collect from a cement works as much cement as possible from Saturday midday through the Sunday. Approximately 500 tons were collected and stored in all sorts of amazing places, including old vaults under the footway by a site cleared before the war, without the owner's knowledge. This supply was almost sufficient to keep the work going when supplemented by the amount allowed under the control,

LONDON CIVIL DEFENCE REGION No.

METROPOLITAN BOROUGH OF ST. PANCRAS

Admit person named below for shelter at

KENTISH TOWN STATION

Name..... Age.....

Address.....

Nature of Employment.....

Date of Issue ·3·42   C. S. BAINBRIDGE,
                                    A.R.P. Controller.

Signature of Issuing Officer.

PERSONS PERMITTED TO USE THIS STATION AS, OR AS A MEANS OF ACCESS TO, AN AIR RAID SHELTER, DO SO AT THEIR OWN RISK IN ALL RESPECTS.

NOT TRANSFERABLE·   FOR FURTHER CONDITIONS OF ISSUE SEE BACK.

National Registration No.

This ticket expires on March 31st, 1942

19 Shelter ticket for Kentish Town Station shelter
As well as 'bunking' (see 18 on p 50) the authorities introduced a ticketing system at popular shelters to ensure that the scarce places were allocated to those in greatest need

(the homeless or those not able to use other shelters). People who already had been issued with an Anderson shelter for their garden would not be high on the list. Note the requirement for the holder's National Identity Card number to minimise fraudulent claims for places.

and only minor delays occurred. The shortage of reinforcing steel was overcome by allowing a firm of Reinforced Concrete Designing Engineers, who had considerable stocks of steel they had bought before the war, to redesign the steel to suit their stock. Their fees for designing had to paid as well as the cost of the steel. This sort of 'headache' with regard to supplies was always occurring, and it was only by ingenious and resourceful methods like those illustrated that the work was kept going. Despite the difficulties, these shelters were completed for less than the estimated cost.

Additional measures were needed to enable a shelter to withstand earth shocks caused by the penetration and explosion of a bomb beneath the earth's surface. The principle was to tie the roof, the walls and the floor together so that each supported the other.[7] Instructions to strengthen shelters throughout the Borough were received at the beginning of August 1941, and in 3 weeks 800 men were at work, mostly transferred from repairing war damage. The work took 9 months to complete and cost about £100,000. Luckily, materials were no longer in short supply.

Tube Stations

Borough Councils had little or nothing to do with the development of two further types of shelter, namely the use of Tube Stations as shelters and the construction of Deep Shelters. About November 1940, at the height of German night attacks on London, public demand that Tube Stations be opened for shelter was so great that, despite Government policy to the contrary, Londoners proceeded to spend the night in stations, taking their own bedding and sleeping on the platforms ([18], p 50).

Maintenance of these shelters was eventually handed over to the Council's Civil Defence Services. Of the eight stations in the Borough, six were used as shelters. In addition, two Deep Shelters[8] were located on the Northern Line. They were in effect 'Communal Hotels' deep underground, being fitted with full washing, recreational and eating facilities.

Part III of the Civil Defence Act 1939 made it compulsory for employers of more than 50 people to provide shelter for their workforce at the place of work, and all schemes had to be submitted to the Local Authority for its approval. Almost 1,000 schemes were submitted and were investigated, approved (with modification if necessary) and inspected upon completion. During the heavy bombing of 1940/41 they were opened after working hours for dormitory use by the public. Councils were empowered to enforce these arrangements by the issue of Defence regulations, but happily, St Pancras had little need to use their powers, thanks to the general cooperation of all those concerned.

The Government bowed to the storm, and the resources of the London Passenger Transport Board were mobilised to cope ([19], p 51).

---

7 The shelters strengthened were the brick surface shelters built in the streets and in urban open spaces. They were strengthened by inserting steel ties to fix the reinforced concrete slab roofs to the walls.

8 The two Deep Shelters in St Pancras, each capable of holding 8,000 people, were those constructed under Camden Town and Goodge Street Underground stations. The former was opened to the public on 16 July 1944 but the latter was retained for use by the military (for General Eisenhower's staff) and thus closed to the public

The Wardens' Service, Fire Guards & Bomb Reconnaissance

Chief Warden and ARP Officer Councillor J E Davies

Following the appointment of an ARP Controller (C S Bainbridge) and full-time ARP Officer, the Wardens' Service was the first of the Civil Defence General Services for the Borough to be formed. The response by residents to an appeal for volunteers was already considerable before the start of hostilities, and when the order was given to engage full-time personnel the preparedness to serve was so great that the number engaged in the first week was three times that of the authorised establishment for the Borough. Headquarters Staff interviews established those who were most suitable to be retained and the Service then rested on sound foundations.

The Wardens' Service included Wardens on the street and Shelter Wardens. It was responsible for the general welfare of the public during and after air attack, and for reporting damage and casualties. The five main features of their work were Local Knowledge, Training, Incident Control, Control of Shelterers and After-Raid Services. When possible, Wardens served in the area where they lived but this was not always possible, so that Wardens had to make themselves thoroughly familiar with the district to which they were appointed. The greatest importance was attached to maintaining detailed census records of occupants of buildings that might be bombed. By facilitating rescue operations this 'census' undoubtedly saved several lives – or relieved much anxiety. Wardens also managed the distribution and three-monthly inspection of gas masks, and in 1942 helped distribute much-needed coal to elderly residents incapable of collecting their fuel.

Training included procedures to alleviate the suffering of people affected by incidents; First Aid, should gas be used; action when communications broke down; duties during Evacuation; and Invasion Defence arrangements. With fresh duties constantly allocated to the Service and new enemy missiles being used, training had to continue to the bitter end.

During the 1940/1941 raids, Supplementary Fire Parties (see below), generally operating under the Wardens' Service, were responsible for dealing with incendiary bombs and incipient fires, and in the latter part of 1941 a certain number of Wardens were transferred to Officer positions in the Fire Guard Service to form a liaison between the two Services.

Incident Officers, 42 at the end of the war, were drawn exclusively from the Wardens' Service after passing a stringent examination. During the fly bomb attacks the Chief Warden and his deputy were appointed Chief Incident Officers.

Over 100 part-time Shelter Wardens maintained the morale and behaviour of shelterers with great tact and understanding, and together with a number of Shelter Marshals at each of the larger Shelters prevented panic on many occasions. In 1943 the Wardens' Service took over the manning of the four Cleansing Stations ([4], p 16) and 186 wardens were trained in Cleansing Station duties at mobile gas cleansing stations ([20], p 54)

In 1940 the authorised paid establishment was 350 personnel, and during the Blitz, 400. Altogether 1,400 people performed effective part-time duty as Wardens during the war.

Fire Prevention (Fire Guard Service)

Before the War the Government advised the public to clear all top floors and roof spaces of inflammable material. Public demonstrations were given in methods of tackling fires, and Wardens were given individual training. Under Section 23 of the Civil Defence Act, 1939, employers of more than 30 persons were required to train a proportion of their employees to fight fires, and local authority instructors trained nominees of business houses in the same way as Wardens.

The larger business houses made their own fire prevention arrangements. Householders were expected to form Stirrup Pump Teams of three persons. Teams had to provide their own equipment until October 1940, when the Ministry of Home Security lent local authorities a limited number (500 to St Pancras) of Stirrup Pumps for the use of volunteers. Wardens undertook to recruit the volunteers and by September 1940 some 1,600 persons had been organised into teams known as Supplementary Fire Parties [21], which proved invaluable in combating incendiary raids on the Borough.

The Fire Watchers Order of September 1940 called on businesses to undertake further duties. However, on the night of 29 December 1940 there was a very severe incendiary attack on central London, and on 18 January 1941 the Minister of Home Security promulgated the first Fire Prevention (Business Premises) Order requiring occupiers of business premises to set up systems to detect and combat IBs[9] and the resultant fires, and the Civil Defence (Compulsory Enrolment) Order, which obliged local authorities to register and enrol male residents in certain age ranges as fire fighters. In March 1941 it was estimated that 40,000 persons were required to cover business premises adequately. Very few of the schemes examined were considered adequate, mainly because of lack of personnel, and in May 1941 the Borough was divided into blocks, each surrounded by streets or other suitable fire breaks, the businesses in each block making a single joint arrangement, thus pooling their manpower resources.

In the residential areas the Wardens' Service had by May 1941 organised over

20 Mobile Gas Cleansing station
The mobile cleansing station was designed to travel to a gas incident for 'on the spot' decontamination of personnel instead of having to move them to the fixed facility (see **[4]**, p 16).

9 Incendiary Bombs, generally small (1-kg) devices dropped in thousands to swamp the defences.

750 Supplementary Fire Parties comprising 2,250 members. After the raids of April–May 1941 it was realised that there would have to be many more volunteers, and at the request of the ARP Emergency Committee the Minister of Home Security applied the Civil Defence (Compulsory Enrolment) Order to the Borough. About 9,000 male British residents between the ages of 18 and 60 years were listed of whom only 2,000 (in addition to the 2,250 volunteers) could actually be enrolled, the remainder claiming exemption on various grounds. In August 1941 the Street Fire Parties were constituted as part of the Wardens' Service and known as the Fire Guard Service.

In August 1942 Fire Guard Duty was also made compulsory for women between the ages of 20 and 45, either at business premises or in street parties. This necessitated a new census of relevant residents to be made, which resulted in the registration of 277 additional men and 6,592 women as fire guards. In October 1943 new Fire Guard Orders came into operation for certain categories of aliens, which produced a further 358 people for duty.

There was, however, a constant drain of personnel through evacuation and call-up and at no time were there more than 12,100

residents available for street fire parties either as volunteers or by compulsory enrolment; of these, a large number were undertaking duty at business premises and therefore entitled to exemption from street duties. It was expected, however, that all fire guards in the residential areas, and many residents not liable for duty, would turn out for incidents in their area. In August 1942 a statutory duty was placed upon fire guards to undertake training. 104 nominees of business areas were trained as Supplementary IB Control Instructors to deliver training in their respective blocks. Lectures were also repeated on 9 successive nights to cover every fire guard on his/her duty night. 46 series of these lectures were delivered. For practical training four fire huts were provided which were used both by day and in the evening.

21 Street Fire Party

The importance of 'fire prevention' had not been adequately appreciated in national ARP planning, but the widespread damage caused by incendiary bombs caused much more effort to be put into fire watching and the better training and equipping of Fire Guards and Street Fire Parties. Here, a three-person team is shown operating a stirrup pump, being aimed by the prone figure. Eventually, across London, some 75% of all fires caused by enemy action were dealt with without the assistance of the National Fire Service.

In the Spring of 1943 the Government introduced Orders under which all Fire Guards – in business and Government premises and in street parties – were welded into one Service under the control of the local authority, the Chief Warden being appointed as Fire Guard Officer, thus forming a tie between the two Services.

The 37 Wardens' Posts were divided into 142 fire sectors, consisting on average of one-sixteenth of a square mile, the boundaries of the Sectors being arranged wherever possible so as not to overlap the Wardens' Post boundaries. The 142 Sectors were then subdivided into approximately 650 blocks, each with a Block or Party Leader in charge, the Sectors being numbered clockwise. Some 42,030 Fire Guards constituted the Fire Guard Service[10], of which one-seventh were on duty each night and sometimes more often.

Theoretical training and practical training and two test exercises held in August and September 1944 led to Regional Commissioners' approval of the organisation in Borough. In the event, however, no serious occasion arose again before VE Day.

The Council provided over 2,000 stirrup pumps to street fire parties together with empty used petrol cans purchased from the Government for the storage of water. Nine Trailer Pumps and nine Wheelbarrow Pumps lent to the Council were also established at the most vulnerable points, and local residents were trained to operate them. For use with the Wheelbarrow Pumps, 162 three-gallon static water tanks were purchased and installed. Many thousands of sandbags and sandmats were distributed around the streets in readiness for immediate use.

Fire-fighting equipment in business and Government premises was the responsibility of the occupiers, who purchased many trailer pumps and stirrup pumps and stored them on their premises in accordance with the requirements of the Order.

From September 1941 occupiers of business premises were required to pay subsistence allowances to all Fire Guards on a Government-approved scale, and were reimbursed through the Council by the Government. Up to June 1945 the Fire Guard Prevention Department processed approximately 30,000 claims for reimbursement.

Bomb reconnaisance

The difficult and dangerous task of making the first investigation of unexploded missiles, prior to report to Group and their disposal by the Royal Engineers' Bomb Disposal section, was undertaken voluntarily throughout the 1940/1941 raids by qualified engineers of the Borough Engineer's Department, but in the latter part of 1941 this duty was divided between the Police and the Qualified Reconnaissance Civil Defence (QRCD) Services. Ten men drawn from the Wardens' Service and the Instructors' Staff were trained and qualified under the supervision of the Royal Engineers' Bomb Disposal Section. Their ready presence undoubtedly saved much valuable time in the designating and handling of every missile.

10 Across the whole country, over five million citizens were involved in Fire Guard duties. In early 1944 the London Regional Commissioner reported that in London "the Fireguard did excellent work in putting out incipient fires.... Some 75% of all fires caused by enemy action have been extinguished by them without the assistance of the National Fire Service".

First Aid Posts

Officer in Charge J M Milburn

n March 1936 a circular was received from the Home Office giving guidance to the Borough Councils in the preparation of First Aid Posts for wartime emergencies. At first it was thought that as school children were likely to be evacuated, the LCC [London County Council] schools would prove suitable, but after nearly six months of negotiation the LCC refused permission and other sites had to be sought. Government advice was that gas was likely to be used and the primary consideration was the organisation of cleansing facilities.

At their first meeting in June, the St Pancras ARP Committee asked the MOH to prepare a report on medical services and to consider using the Prince of Wales Road Baths, Highgate Library and the British Medical Association building as first aid posts.

In September 1936, classes began to be formed to teach first aid, first under the auspices of the St John and British Red Cross organisations, later directly controlled by the Borough Council. Hundreds of people were trained, but much of this effort was lost because so much time elapsed before the service became necessary.

In May 1938 it was decided in the light of ARP Memo 7 that the number of volunteer staff in St Pancras first aid posts should be 256, half men and half women, and as a preliminary arrangement, there should be four first aid posts situated at:-
(a) LCC Lido, Parliament Hill Fields
(b) Cecil Sharp House, Gloucester Road
(c) Prince of Wales Road Baths
(d) Royal Veterinary College, Royal College Street.

After meetings between the Borough and the hospitals, 55 doctors offered to assist when necessary.

During the Munich crisis five emergency first aid posts were designated: the Avalon Nursing Home, Prince of Wales Road Baths, Town Hall basement, Plender Street Baths and Whitfield Street Baths.

A committee of ten volunteers was formed in each of these places to advise the MOH of further necessary steps. Cleansing facilities for gas were still the main consideration in these places rather than dealing with lightly injured casualties.

In October 1938 the MOH reported that because of the absence of medical officers, nurses and equipment, and because these temporary posts were not near hospitals, they would not be functional, particularly with seriously wounded cases; and the position in regard to ambulances was unclear, as both the Borough and the LCC were earmarking lorries for conversion into ambulances. The temporary posts were then abandoned and first aid posts were established at each of the eight hospitals in St Pancras.

In January 1939 the staffing for the posts was fixed at 110 men and 550 women, total 660; of these, some 350 volunteers had been enrolled, of whom 135 had been trained.

In March 1939 we considered how injured people could be treated at the actual incident, and at our request the Ministry agreed that two Mobile Medical Units should be established using two ordinary furniture vans for the purpose ([22], p 58). It was presumed that personnel for these units would have come from the first aid post volunteers, who by June 1939 totalled 573, of whom 200 had been trained in first aid.

At the end of August 1939 authority was given for the first time that full-time mebers of the ARP services could be paid – £3 per week for men and £2 for women – and this was extended to personnel on the Mobile Medical Units (6 men and 12 women per unit).

In theory these first aid posts were to be used as sorting stations to avoid overcrowding in the main hospitals. The lightly injured were to be treated and retained in the first aid post and the more seriously injured transferred to the hospital. In practice, this was never implemented, partly because the men in the Stretcher

Party Service were trained to decide the destination of the patient and partly because the number of casualties fell far short of the estimated numbers likely to arise from bombing.

Until September 1940 training was regularly maintained, but as this could not occupy 12 hours per shift the personnel were allowed to work in the casualty departments of the adjoining hospitals, with the double purpose of assisting the hospital and training our personnel. During the Blitz of 1940 few casualties were dealt with at the first aid posts – averaging just over 100 a month in the eight posts – or in the hospitals. This was quite contrary to general expectations based on experience of the bombing in Spain, and was no doubt due to the extent of advice given to the general population in the taking of simple air raid precautions and protection from blast. As the casualty figures were so low, the volunteers who for various reasons resigned were not replaced.

In general, the Mobile Medical Units did not function as intended because (a) the number of casualties at one spot was seldom high, (b) the lightly injured casualties found their way to first aid posts and hospitals, and (c) the Borough has a large number of hospitals – except on the one occasion when St Pancras Hospital was bombed and our first aid post virtually destroyed, fortunately without loss of life amongst the nurses. One of the medical units with doctor, trained nurse and seven auxiliary nurses promptly proceeded to set up a first aid post in a public air raid shelter nearby. They were able to do good work.

As raiding had almost ceased it was decided early in 1942 that the first aid posts attached to hospitals should be merged with the hospitals, and many of the staff were then released for other duties. This left four independent first aid posts, at St Margaret's ([5], p 18), the Royal Veterinary College, the Girls' Orphanage and Bayham Street. In December 1944 Bayham Street was transferred to the Hampstead General Hospital and the posts at the Royal Veterinary College and the Girls' Orphanage were closed, leaving only one at St Margaret's, where the staff were retained until 30 June 1945.

22 The St Pancras Mobile Medical Unit used a converted furniture van, but the facility was eventually abandoned because so many hospitals were available in the Borough. The MMU is shown here on an exercise dealing with their 'patient' on a stretcher.

Heavy Rescue Service (LCC)

Officers Mr H Watkinson and Mr F C Turner

In 1938 all District Surveyors in London volunteered to organise a Heavy Rescue Service in the event of war, and about 6 weeks before war broke out they were called to County Hall to receive an outline of the suggested organisation. Mr H G May[11] reported on the organisation of the Immediate Action Parties (Rescue) recruited from the builders in the Borough.

Like the Ambulance Service, the Rescue Service was administered by the London County Council. It was largely recruited from the LCC Architects' Department under the technical direction of the appropriate District Surveyor. In St Pancras, most of the men were local residents or employees of local building firms. Some builders, namely G Rodwell, W O Barns and F G Gregory, stuck to the service throughout and became valuable officers.

In the early days tools and equipment were scarce. Acetylene flares were part of the equipment but were hardly ever used, as objections were continually raised by police and the public; consequently, lighting at all incidents prior to June 1944 was very poor and it was amazing how much good work was done under such bad conditions. The strength of the Service in those early days was 400 men, divided into 40 parties, 20 parties being on duty at one time for 24 hours, the remaining 20 parties resting at home. The first few weeks saw the issue of protective clothing, the requisition of rescue vehicles, the issue of working tackle and tools, and putting the Service on a fighting footing should air raids commence. The first twelve months were mainly employed in training, in the adaptation of vehicles, improvements at the four depots and other peaceful tasks. Happy those summer days at Cromer Street and Hilldrop Road (training centres)! How many pseudo casualties were lowered from first floor windows, heaved over 10-foot walls, or retrieved from bottomless basements, by all manner of ingenious devices – and all performed without a single real casualty, although there were times when someone's heart missed a beat or two. In August 1940 in the Regional Rescue Competition, Rescue Leader Alf Tudor and his party stationed at William Ellis Depot walked through the Borough trials, swept up the Group One trials (and a trophy) and passed on to the Regional Final at Crystal Palace, to lose the Regional Cup by an unfortunate misunderstanding on Alf's part.

However, this playfulness came to an end. The Service faced its first grim task on the night of 7/8 September 1940, when the Borough Controller received instructions to send help to Oriental Road, Silvertown. Four rescue parties went out to their baptism of fire, two from Malet Place and one each from Bartholomew Road and Bangor Wharf depots (see p 10). That night's experience has been the topic of conversation in the depots ever since. The first real test in St Pancras came on the night of 9/10 September, when parties were sent to incidents in Allcroft Road, Harrington Square, Argyle Street etc., and night after night followed in similar vein. Parties turned out to incidents, sometimes twice in the same night, did their job, and returned to Depot to await the next call. Often they worked all night, and handed over to the incoming shift, tasks not completed, next morning.

Much fine work was done during those days by individual and collective effort. The first land mine was lowered by Tom Boulter and party from the roof of a house in Harrington Square ('Don't be frightened' said the RN official, 'it's 90% safe'); another land mine was removed

11 An engineer with Mathews & Sons, 72 Tottenham Court Road, in December 1938 Mr May offered to organise the Rescue and Demolition Parties for the Borough – his offer was accepted by a grateful Borough Council.

from Kelvinators in Gray's Inn Road, and there was an occasion in Stanhope Street when rescue operations continued almost on top of an unexploded bomb. The rescue work done at Byron Court, at Argyle and Birkenhead Streets and at Harrington Square won a George Medal for Jock Stewart and little A G Palmer (see p 19), and a commendation for Len Bryant. At the Prince of Wales Road incident that grand old warrior F G Gregory earned and won the British Empire Medal. On two vicious nights in April and May 1941, incidents in Pratt Street, Haverstock Hill, Wellesley Road and Mackworth Street, yielded British Empire Medals for Ted Harris, W Horton, Charlie Thorogood and Eddie Smith (see p 89).

On rare occasions during the first Blitz we had to call on outside assistance, but the Borough Service generally handled its own incidents, and moreover often went to help neighbouring districts: during those fateful days and nights St Pancras vehicles and parties were seen in Paddington, St Marylebone and Kensington.

In addition to rescue operations [23], the Service carried out work such as the shoring up of properties, the demolition of dangerous ones and the salvage of furniture and effects. Luckily, it sustained no fatal casualties – narrow escapes, yes, but no one lost his life during the execution of his duty. Many happy relations were forged between the Service and the public: the rescued often visited the rescuer afterwards to tender his or her thanks.

The night of 10/11 May was followed by a long lull until raids recommenced in January 1943. Training was resumed, of course without the early enthusiasm of 1941, but the work consisted mostly of tidying up the mess, the demolition of dangerous buildings, the clearance of sites and the erection of guard walls around them.

During this period we lost many of our old-timers to the Forces, and as a result

23 Heavy Rescue Party with listening apparatus built by one of the St Pancras Wardens for use in searching for survivors in debris. A rescue exercise at a bomb-damaged property in NW5 (corner of Lupton Street and Brecknock Road).

the average age of the personnel climbed to 40-50. Mutual aid between Boroughs was brought to a high standard; Group Mobile Rescue squads were equipped with 7-ton cranes, debris lorries and, in emergency, narrow-gauge railway track and bogies. The benefit of this augmentation was felt at the Birkenhead Street incident on 18 October 1943, when operations were completed in 62 hours. The stretcher parties had by now been trained to operate as Light Rescue Parties. Members of the National Fire Service were trained for rescue work, and brought with them their lighting and other special equipment.

Such was the set-up of the Rescue Services when the fly bomb made its first appearance on the night of the 15/16 June 1944, in Clarence Way, Kentish Town. For the first time the full scheme was put into operation, the Borough Heavy and Light Rescue Parties forming the nucleus, augmented by the Group Mobile Squad with their crane and lorry fleet and by the NFS[12] with their mobile lighting equipment. Relaxation of the lighting restrictions at incidents enormously facilitated the handling of these large-scale incidents. This fly bomb fell at 11.45 p.m. on 15 June and the last casualty was accounted for at 11.07 p.m. on 16 June, less than 24 hours later.

At the end of 1944 came the last cut in numbers. On 18 December 1944 the operational strength was reduced to 18 parties of 7 men each, 9 parties on duty at one time. From an 'on duty' strength in 1939 of 20 parties of 10 men, average age 30, the Service was eventually reduced to 9 parties of 7 men each, average age 50.

On 1 July 1945 the Service was disbanded. Many have come and gone during these years. To all who have passed through, whether scholars, roaders, wharfers or placers, we wish good luck on their return to 'Civvy Street'.

12 National Fire Service. In August 1941, as a result of the experience during the Blitz, local Fire Brigades (including the highly respected London Fire Service) were nationalised to ensure common standards and drills and to make best use of experienced senior fire incident officers.

Light Rescue Parties
(First Aid Parties; Stretcher Parties)

Officer in Charge Mr J H Milburn (1937-1945)

The organisation of First Aid Parties was authorised in March 1936. In September 1937 classes in First Aid began, first under the auspices of the St John and British Red Cross, but later under the direct control of the Borough Council. The training of men as parties rather than individuals started in August 1938 in one of the London University buildings in Malet Place. By August 1939 there were 400 trained men, 250 untrained, and a further number being recruited. The authorised establishment at the time was 610 men. The first batch of 'graduates' entered service on 31 August 1939, stationed at the Depots at Malet Place, Old William Ellis School, Bartholomew Road and Inverness Street in 12-hour shifts. The men on night duty were expected to stand by all night and therefore had no bunks. They had a boiler suit for uniform, and large furniture vans as vehicles. Included in the equipment were stretchers and blankets, in which the men used to sleep at night. During training the parties worked for a while at the St Pancras Mortuary, where they learned to handle the dead, a lesson that proved invaluable during the Blitz. After a few weeks the 12-hour system was abandoned in favour of a 24-hour system which remained in operation until the end. Shifts changed at 8 a.m., and meals and sleeping accommodation were provided at the depots. When the duties of men in the 'First Aid Parties' were extended to include stretcher-carrying, they became 'Stretcher Parties'.

The first incidents in St Pancras on the night of 9 September 1940 included two major ones at Harrington Square and Allcroft Road, where the bomb dropped near the depot and the Stretcher Parties with the Heavy Rescue Squads rushed across the road and got to work. So it went on night after night, terminating with the biggest raid in May 1941. The parties would turn out at once, no matter how heavy a raid was in progress, and frequently carried on when they could have been relieved. Many of the members of the squads would turn out on the nights when they were off duty to give a hand wherever they could. The Stretcher Parties had some gruesome tasks to perform, working under difficult conditions, but always carried on and were a great credit to the Borough.

The personal equipment of the Parties was gradually increased, and each man was supplied with a blue battledress, boots and beret. Before this the men had a boiler suit and gas clothing, the latter worn during the whole 12 hours on duty without discomfort, though in their gas training they had been told that the gas suits could not be worn for more than two or three hours. In addition proper dormitories were arranged, wooden bunks provided and blankets issued.

In March 1942 the Service became the 'Light Rescue Service' and equipment similar to that carried by the Heavy Rescue Service was supplied. Prior to this the stretcher parties had not been allowed to clear sites or remove debris from casualties, but stood by until the Heavy Rescue Service had uncovered the victims; now it was considered that the men should take on the wider duties of searching buildings, tunnelling, etc., and work on the same basis as the Heavy Rescue Service. During the lull period the Parties were employed in handling wounded servicemen arriving at the main-line railway stations, in demolishing houses unfit for habitation, in clearance of blitzed sites, and in recovering 63 Anderson Shelters from blitzed sites. An incident occurred at Birkenhead Street in October 1943 when the old Stretcher Parties made their first appearance as the Light Rescue Service. At a later stage when the VI attack started, the Light Rescue Service did further good work, and proved the value of the changeover from Stretcher Parties to Light Rescue parties.

Because many medical men had been called up, it was impossible to have doctors regularly attending at the depots for the training, and after the initial course in First Aid the extension of training was carried out by our own leaders. This included the selection by examination of those to be leaders of the parties as well as supervisors of the depots. New recruitment and training had to be continuous, as many of the men originally recruited had left for other work or the Forces, and we never reached the staffing of 610 authorised by the Home Office. However, the number of men we did have enabled us to form about 45 parties on each shift, and this was sufficient for all the calls received. As the raiding decreased, establishment was reduced to 430, then in October 1943 to 208, in August 1944 to 160, and in December 1944 to 80.

Gas Identification Service

Officers S Jacobs, M D S Lewis, G Miles, R Llewellyn

n 1937 the Home Office organised the Gas Detection and Identification Service, with Mr S Jacobs in charge. During October 1939 the service was renamed as the Gas Identification Service. At the first London University special course on the subject in November 1939, the above-named men qualified as Gas Identification Officers (GIOs) and were posted to St Pancras. Messrs Jacobs and Lewis served continuously until 'D' Day. In most local authorities GIOs were on call and had to be fetched by car when required, but in St Pancras, at the request of the Controller, the GIOs were asked to do a shift in the Control Room, spending the night at the Town Hall under the same conditions as the rest of the voluntary staff, and they continued to do this until the end of the war in Europe. When a report of poison gas was received in the Control Room, the GIO would go to the spot to ascertain the presence and nature of the gas reported, despatch a report to the Control Room, take a sample of the gas or contaminated material to be forwarded to the Senior Gas Adviser (London Region) if required; he then advised the services operating on the site as to the extent and duration of the danger. Although the enemy never did use poison gas, the GIO did valuable work in giving lectures to each Wardens' Post and Control Room Staff, and latterly explained to the Wardens' Service the use of the Pocket Vapour detector.

On a few occasions the assistance of a GIO was required, for instance when a bag of red powder was found in the street and brought to the Town Hall for investigation. It was identified as a 'dye bag' containing a fluorescent substance used by German airmen to reveal their position if shot down in the sea.

When the Gas Identification Service was disbanded Dr E F Armstrong, Chief Chemical Adviser to the Ministry of Home Security, stated "there are grounds for considering that the strength of the country's defence against gas attack from the air has been a potent factor in deterring the enemy from using gas. Towards which the Gas Identification Service has contributed its full share."

The following were members of the Service: Messrs R Bidgood, L A Harris, S Jacobs, M D S Lewis, R Llewellyn, G Miles, V D Pole, J A Stewart, I A Thomas, K J Verrile, A Whitnell, H J Williams, and L H Woolgrove.

Ambulance Service

A G Hillman, Director, London Ambulance Service (LCC)

The London County Council had the responsibility to provide a Civil Defence Ambulance Service. As they already operated the London Ambulance Service in peacetime, it was a simple matter to form the London Auxiliary Service, with their own experienced officers to supervise the work. In St Pancras there were seven Ambulance Stations under the supervision of Mr J Rees:

Temporary Ambulance Stations in St Pancras

Station No.	Address	Closed
T.S.5	Pratt Street	1/7/45
49	102 St Pancras Way	31/11/42
50	20/22 William Road	5/2/45
51	Starcross Street	8/7/43
54	Malden Road	28/8/41
55 [see p 45]	St Albans Road	24/12/41
NW Auxiliary	Lawn Road NW3	1/7/45

The Group Ambulance Officer was responsible to London Regional HQ for the operation of the service and kept a close watch on the movement of the ambulances. All these stations were under the immediate charge of the ARP Controller, and ambulances were ordered out in the same way as the Stretcher Parties or Heavy Rescue Parties. When an ambulance or sitting car was used for civilian purposes the Control Room had to be informed of its movements. Station 50 was an 'Indian Station', having a Station Officer in charge who had lived in India for 25 years and spoke a number of local languages. In the early days three members of this station were well-known doctors. The members were very proud of being the only Indian Ambulance Station in London.

The Ambulance Service was quite different from other services, as the members (men and women) lived in the Station or nearby; they went out when called on at any time, no matter how heavy the raid was, straight to the incident, and frequently standing by under heavy fire. Cooperation with the Stretcher Parties was always excellent. Before leaving the station the Ambulance Drivers were told where the casualties were to be taken – often to hospitals outside the Borough. One Ambulance Station had to be evacuated four times. On one occasion they moved to a nearby square, parked the vehicles by a public telephone kiosk, rang the Control Room and kept the line engaged so that they could keep in touch until the All Clear.

During the Blitz, Station 51 had several midwives among the staff. One night the station received an urgent maternity call. The ambulance collecting the case was returning along Tottenham Court Road when it had to pull up, and a fine baby girl was delivered, under a sky full of planes, bursting shells and falling shrapnel. The ambulance proceeded to the Maternity Hospital. On arrival the hospital staff seized the stretcher and rushed the patient into the Maternity Ward. The ambulance attendant followed with the baby carefully wrapped up. On reaching the ward Matron asked her in a most superior tone "What do you want?" The attendant replied "Just to give the mother her baby daughter." The first news the Control Room heard of this event was an excited Station Officer ringing up, saying "It's a girl, it's a girl."

On one occasion a fire station was badly damaged by a land mine, and some firemen were trapped in the basement. One of them managed to telephone to Control on the direct line and gave directions as to the best way to rescue them. The Rescue Parties got to work, and ambulances were sent to collect the casualties. The Ambulance Station Officer reported that they had removed two badly injured firemen, one unconscious and the other with his face very badly smashed, yet in this terrible condition insisting on giving full particulars about himself and his unconscious comrade.

On the night of 15/16 October 1940 Control received 24 calls for ambulances or cars to be used for accidents, evacuation, etc. This was apart from Civil Defence requirements.

The CD Ambulance personnel served the people of St Pancras not only during air raids but in various ambulance and ancillary functions throughout the war; their presence was a real source of strength in supplementing the regular Ambulance service, which was facing the common wartime staff shortages, etc. The auxiliaries undertook a large number of movements of sick people to general hospitals, conveyed doctors, midwives and medical stores, and took physically disabled children to and from school.

Women's Legion Drivers

Mrs L Johnstone-Wilson

The Women's Legion, an organisation authorised by the War Office to wear khaki uniform, seconded a number of the Corps to St Pancras. All experienced drivers, they were employed to drive the Control Car, Mobile Canteen and Utility Van, beginning in the early days of the Blitz in 1940. Five drivers, on 24-hour on-call shifts, were used. Meals and sleeping accommodation were provided at the Town Hall.

The Mobile Canteen [24] supplied refreshments and food to Rescue Parties engaged in Rescue work or working on damaged sites after a raid. It was sent out at regular intervals during both day and night. The Control Car was available during the night to take the Borough Engineer or his representative to incidents during a raid. The Utility Van was fitted with a listening apparatus used to locate people trapped under debris ([23] p 60), and would be taken out when required. Jobs were cheerfully carried out while a raid was in progress. The arrival of the Canteen was always very welcome at an incident, and the work of the drivers was much appreciated.

Duties continued until the end of July 1945, and the drivers carried on until the end of August.

The following members served in St Pancras: Mrs E Barff, Mrs Christie, Mrs S Davies, Mrs Gribble, Miss F Holmes, Mrs L Johnstone-Wilson, Miss Jean Simpson, Miss S Treadgold, Miss Joan Williams.

24 CD workers using the Mobile Canteen
The arrival at an incident of the Mobile Canteen supplying hot and cold food and drinks greatly assisted and cheered CD workers at the bomb scene, where the work often continued for several days and nights.

Decontamination and Repair Services

Office in Charge Harold C Cons (Assistant Surveyor)

The Decontamination squads were one of the Civil Defence Services which happily were not needed for decontamination, but because they were also trained as Road and Sewer repair gangs they saw much active service in the repair of roads, sewers and bridges damaged by enemy action, and particularly in the clearance of debris from the streets. This work of clearance, barricading, and placing red danger lamps on unusable roads went on day and night throughout the war, particularly during the 1940/41 Blitz, and again during the fly bomb and long-range rocket periods. It was a point of honour amongst the men that a road should be opened to traffic at the earliest possible minute after the fall of the missile.

The expenditure on War Damage Repairs to roads and clearance of debris in St Pancras was more than £205,000 and on sewer repairs £12,000 (80 separate sewers). Contractors were brought in to assist in the work, but most of it was carried out by the Council's own workmen.

The Decontamination and Repair Squads first came into being in the last months of 1938, and in January 1939 a comprehensive report on the organisation, training and operational details of the service in the event of war was submitted to and approved by the Council.

The squads were formed on a voluntary basis from the men of the Highways Department, and training was carried out after normal working hours. Very early in the history of Civil Defence the Home Office, and afterwards the Ministry of Home Security, decided that although the Decontamination Squads were a designated ARP service, the road repair squads were not. It was always a sore point that whilst working as repair parties or in the clearance of debris, they were not officially recognised as part of the Civil Defence organisation. Towards the end of the war, however, whilst working on incidents they were treated as members of the Civil Defence organisation in respect of canteen facilities. This was, I know, greatly appreciated by all concerned.

In January and February 1939 men did not volunteer in sufficient numbers, (a) because decontamination was a new departure for them and they knew nothing about such work, and (b) because they thought there would be no war anyway, so why waste time preparing for something that wouldn't happen. As a result of many meetings, enough men were persuaded to volunteer, and they become enthusiastic.

The wartime establishment strength of the service was decided by the Home Office in January 1939 and was to be 22 squads of seven men with a 50% reserve. There were not sufficient fit men under the age of 45 available on the staff of the Department to form this number of squads, but by the beginning of 1939 20 squads of 7 men each, together with drivers and transport, had been formed. A total of 163 men volunteered for this work, all keen to get on with the training, which occurred after normal working hours.

Looking back on those early days of training brings many memories, some humorous, but at the time not quite so pleasant. We were beginning something that was to most of us entirely new. There was no precedent for anything we did, and apart from learning the main principles of decontamination, we had to experiment and find out for ourselves the best way of tackling the job. Like most of the ARP services in those days, there was little equipment available, and many of the tools and appliances for training purposes had to be improvised from existing materials. We even had to make our own standpipes and keys. It was not until March 1940 that standpipes were supplied, and the only hoses available at the time were second-hand, mostly worn-out fire hoses. When they did arrive they had no couplings, and when a hose was put into use, many were the holes and splits in the canvas that appeared – and consequently, many the thorough dousings we all got.

Training in decontamination at first involved the 'wet method': liquid persisting from a gas attack on horizontal surfaces was to be thoroughly hosed with water, then scrubbed with a stiff long-handled brush, while vertical surfaces (walls, edges of kerbs, etc.) were given a coat of bleach paste and left to 'weather'. At the end of 1941 a dry bleach method was introduced, which was much simpler and less arduous. The bleach powder was simply sprinkled over contaminated surfaces and left to 'weather'. The first practical lessons were given in the Highways depot, away from the eye of the public. Soon, however, the men settled down into the routine and were then taken out on the streets – then the fun started.

The mere sighting of lorries carrying squads of men dressed in protective clothing was the signal for all the small boys of the neighbourhood, and many grown-ups as well, to congregate and watch the proceedings. Sites in some of the quieter streets such as Park Village East, Hampshire Street NW5 and Wrotham Road NW1 were chosen for training purposes, and although the sites were changed each night, a crowd invariably gathered and got in the way of the squads, passing uncomplimentary remarks, particularly when the worn-out hoses burst and held up proceedings. However, the men took the remarks in good part. Possibly, the occasions when a coupling came apart and drenched the onlookers were not always accidents!

Between January and September 1939 the 20 squads were trained in decontamination work, while a number of gangers and other men were formed into a nucleus for the road repair squads. As road repair was their normal work, little training was required. Each squad attended for 2 hours of training on one evening every fortnight. Drills were held on four nights each week, two or three squads attending each night. In addition to individual and squad training, many exercises were held in combination with the other ARP Services, the Police and the Fire Brigade.

On 28 August 1939, mobilisation of the squads began, equipment and the final wartime instructions were issued.

The decontamination repair squads then numbered 400 men. The squads were put on full-time duty at the four ARP Depots, with 3 Decontamination Squads and 3 Repair Squads at each of the Depots at Inverness Street, Old William Ellis School and Malet Place, and 2 Decontamination Squads and 2 Repair Squads at the Bartholomew Road Depot. At each depot the squads were under the control of a District Foreman with a Street Inspector as deputy, and the men worked in 12-hour shifts.

In the early days of the war conditions at the depots were poor. There seemed to be a deficiency of everything – blankets, mattresses, beds and washing facilities – in fact, for many nights the men slept on the floor. There were many grumbles and complaints. Before many days had passed things began to settle down into a routine, and conditions steadily improved.

It soon became clear that the major part of the outside staff of the Highways department could not be kept standing-by inactive at the depots, particularly as the expected raids did not materialise, and on 11 September 1939 the number of full-time squads standing by was reduced to one Decontamination and one Repair Squad, the remaining men returning to normal work, required to report to their depot when an air-raid warning sounded. By the end of September the squads standing by were further reduced to a night shift only, and two or three weeks later all men returned to normal duty.

During the whole time the men were on 12-hour shifts they received no overtime pay, only their normal week's wages, and although many requests were made to Regional HQ for authority to pay something extra for the long hours worked, it was never given, this naturally causing much dissension. A number of meetings and discussions were held, but to no avail, and the men never forgot the time when they stood by for nothing.

When all had returned to normal work, Repair Squads from the night sweepers took over the night work. These men, 8 of them on duty at one time, bore the brunt of the night bombing raids. The night repair parties worked in two shifts under the direction of a Night Street Inspector – 5 p.m. to 1 a.m. and 12 midnight to 8 a.m., but during heavy raids the first shift often stayed on to help. The night squads' duties were very diverse, particularly in the early days of the Blitz. The primary task was to place ropes and red lamps across roads rendered impassable to traffic by craters and debris. They also put out the fires caused by incendiary bombs that fell on the Inverness Street Depot and surrounding precinct, removed the dead to the Mortuary – before Mortuary Vans were in operation – cleared debris from the streets, assisted in rescue work, and were generally the utility men of Civil Defence.

A few anecdotes concerning the episodes encountered, humorous as well as tragic, follow.

We were out early one morning during a raid, looking for a reported unexploded shell, when suddenly less than 50 yards away a parachute mine exploded on some houses. We were all flung to the ground, and when we had picked ourselves up, I shouted "Is everybody all right?" "No, we aren't", said a shaky voice in the dark. Making our way to where the man was, we found him sitting on the kerb, holding his leg. We asked where he was injured. 'Injured, be ......' he replied, 'who's going to pay for my torn trousers?'

One night we had just cleared the debris in a street and were on the point of returning to the depot, when a loud knocking was heard from a badly blasted house. One of the men called through a door which appeared to be wedged shut, and on getting no reply he pushed the door in, to be met by an irate old lady who said she had been trying to fix the door, so that she could get some sleep – now, not only had she to put up with bombs, but hooligans as well.

On another occasion the squad had spent some time clearing debris from Camden High Street; after much hard work the traffic was able to proceed once more. After giving a last look round, the men mounted their lorry and drove away. They had gone about 100 yards when another bomb dropped and blew the heaped-up debris, and some more as well, back across the road, undoing all their work. The language of the returning squad was unprintable for a minute or two. Then they set to work and started over.

After a night raid the repair gangs had to go hard at it all day clearing up the debris, and making temporary repairs to roads and sewers. The men were getting very little rest or sleep owing to the incessant raiding, so it was decided that the night work would be left entirely to designated night gangs – the day men reporting at daybreak and getting to work before the normal traffic commenced.

During the main Blitz period from September 1940 to May 1941, none of us got enough sleep or rest. We worked all through daylight on repairs, and snatched odd hours of sleep during the night as best we could, usually partly dressed so as to be ready for any emergency. Then at daylight I would instruct the District Foremen where to concentrate their men and equipment to the best advantage.

Ten to fifteen separate incidents each night were quite common, of which about three-quarters involved damage to roads and/or sewers, as well as strewing debris about that had to be cleared. Then there were thousands of incendiary bombs which caused many fires, all of which also produced debris.

It is amazing that more men were not killed by collision with other vehicles. It seemed that the mere sight of a number of vehicles going along a street during a night raid called down the wrath of 'Jerry' in the shape of bombs. However much we reduced our car lights, they were still visible to the airmen above. So for much of the time vehicles were going to incidents with no lights at all. It's a wonder there were not serious road accidents every night, but there were not.

This was with a few exceptions the period of small bombs. A different technique had to be adopted in later days, when fly bombs and long-range rockets appeared.

A typical incident of how the men got on with the job may be given by quoting a night in September 1941 when a bomb caused a crater in Kentish Town Road between Caversham Road and Islip Road School. Other bombs were dropped immediately to the east and west of the road (no doubt aimed at the main Midland Railway lines), and the whole of Kentish Town Road between Prince of Wales Road and Leighton Road was covered in glass, bricks, slates, and timber, rendering the road wholly impassable to vehicular traffic. By 9 a.m. next morning the debris had been cleared and the road opened to normal traffic. No road in the Borough was at any time kept closed for more than a few hours, unless the crater was so large as to occupy the majority of the carriageway, there were unexploded bombs or dangerous buildings in the street. It was a major task to keep Control notified of the road block situation, as the position changed hourly.

A most useful appliance for clearing streets of debris was the motor broom; without their aid streets could not have been cleared so quickly.

During the worst of the Blitz, repair of damaged roads in the Borough was a serious problem. For weeks at a time it seemed that for every incident cleared, two more occurred. Even the combined resources of the Borough's men with the expert public works contractors (Davis Contractors, G Percy Trentham and to a smaller extent Edmund Nuttals) could not keep pace with the damage.

Despite the existence of a mutual assistance scheme whereby Group Headquarters arranged for parties of men from other Boroughs to go to the aid of a badly hit Borough, all the adjoining Boroughs that might have helped us were as badly hit as ourselves, or worse. Men could be sent from another Borough to help us on only one occasion, and it is a source of great satisfaction that we were able to keep communications open by our own unaided efforts.

One of the greatest difficulties during this time was the acute shortage of plant, particularly pumps and compressors. On several occasions the contractors had to bring equipment into the Borough from as far away as Bristol. The lack of plant for handling large-diameter concrete sewer pipes was so acute that we designed and made in the Council workshops two travelling gantries capable of lifting pipes weighing up to 10 cwt each, and these were used continuously for many months.

When the Regional plant scheme was formed, in which each Borough produced plant on behalf of the government and for which 100% reimbursement was given, each Borough undertook to maintain the plant to supply to the drivers, and to make it available to other Boroughs in time

of need. St Pancras then purchased two compressors, two 15-cwt cranes and one 2-ton crane, two concrete mixers, a chaseside shovel and a number of pumps of various sizes, all of which we and other Boroughs used extensively.

Another scheme instituted during the Blitz period by London Region to relieve the acute labour shortage was the 'Fisher' Scheme inaugurated by Sir Warren Fisher, in which short-term deferment of call-up into the Armed Forces was granted to masons, paviors, gangers and labourers engaged on war damage repairs. The scheme remained in operation until the peak period of repairs had passed. It is unimaginable that we could have carried on during that time without such a scheme.

After May 1941, when the continuous raiding stopped, and until June 1944, when fly bombs commenced, only isolated raids were experienced. Although some of the damage done during these raids was severe it was easier to handle, as the lull between raids enabled us to catch up with the work.

Acting in the spirit of mutual assistance St Pancras Road Repair Services on several occasions assisted other Boroughs. Notable was the raid on East and West Ham in early September 1940. On this occasion two motor brooms travelled all the way from St Pancras to West Ham, where their services were urgently required.

The occasion of the very heavy incendiary and high explosives raid on Fulham on the night of 20 February 1944 was the acme of aid from St Pancras to another Borough. During the early morning of 21 February, the Control Room was told that Fulham had been very badly hit. Soon after came a call for all assistance that could be sent. Instructions were immediately sent out to all men at Inverness Street Depot. By 7.30 a.m. 110 men together with lorries, tools and plant were sent – a self-contained unit able to undertake anything, including sewer repairs. District Foreman Houlan was detailed to go with the men and to remain in charge at Fulham.

Because of reports that most of the roads surrounding the stricken area were congested, application was made to Scotland Yard for a route and a guide – they promptly arranged the route, and sent two motor-cyclist policemen to escort the convoy of vehicles. Promptly at 7.45 a.m., the convoy moved off from the depot and, shepherded by the police, very soon arrived at Fulham. The men immediately set to work clearing debris and it was quickly apparent that our help was very timely indeed. The men remained at Fulham for several days, and assisted in the clearance of debris, repair of roads and sewers.

The type of HE bomb used on Fulham was much larger than in previous raids. Although our primary task was to assist Fulham, the experience gained was extremely valuable when it came to handling the larger incidents caused by fly bombs and long-range rockets, which were soon to follow. The Acting ARP Controller of Fulham later wrote to the Borough Engineer of St Pancras: "Please convey my warmest thanks to all your personnel who rendered assistance to Fulham CD Services during the raid on Sunday night 20.2.44 and subsequently. Reports from my officers in the field have been full of the highest praise for the efficient and enthusiastic manner in which the duties were undertaken."

During the whole of the war **Decontamination Squads** had to be maintained to an efficient standard, as it was never certain whether or when gas would be used. With the exception of the Blitz period, and at times of other heavy damage, squad training went on at regular intervals during the war. Many combined exercises were also held and although some had to be abandoned because of air raids, they were on the whole successful and instructive. Much valuable assistance was given by Robert Lee, MIEE AMI MechE, Chief Electrical Engineer and Manager, who acted as Gas Coordinating Officer for the various sections of Decontamination.

It was hard to keep the squads up to strength because of the call-up, but with the advent of the 'dry bleach' method [25] of decontamination at the end of 1941, the work became less arduous and older men could be employed − at the beginning

25 Decontamination Party using bleach powder in Hawley Road, Camden Town
The initial intention for the treatment of streets and properties that had been subject to gas attack was decontamination by hosing them down with water, but the later introduction of 'bleaching powder' for the task was greatly welcomed by the Decontamination Teams.

of the war the average age of men in the Decontamination Service was 37, in 1945 it was 50, the total number being much the same as in 1939.

Transporting the squads presented a problem. There were not enough suitable lorries available, so existing vehicles had to be adapted: platforms were fitted on the S&D Freighters used for the collection of dustbins. The gulley wagons were fitted with pumps to supply water and with platforms to accommodate the squad and its appliances. All this work was carried out by the Council's blacksmiths, carpenters and so on during the turmoil of the war. Suffolk Wharf was fitted up with water pipes, taps, hose pipes, etc., for the decontamination of vehicles, and in addition sites in Regent's Park, Cumberland Market and a number of little-used side streets were earmarked in which contaminated vehicles could be parked whilst 'weathering'. Firms in the borough that owned many vehicles were invited to participate in a mutual aid scheme. Each of the firms agreed to train squads in vehicle decontamination and if there were a gas attack, the driver of a contaminated vehicle would, after preliminary treatment, take his vehicle to the nearest garage owned by a member of the scheme and be decontaminated there. This scheme would have enabled urgently needed vehicles, such as those engaged on the distribution of food and other necessities, to be returned to normal work without delay.

In the early days of the war some hundreds of gas detection surfaces were prepared all over the borough. The detector surface consisted of areas about 12 inches square, painted with a special paint on the tops of pillar boxes, electricity feeder boxes, etc., and in some cases on specially erected boards. Any droplets of mustard gas would leave a reddish brown stain on this painted surface. They had to be repainted about every four months throughout the war.

An event which gave much satisfaction to the personnel was the issue of uniforms, thus bringing the service into line with other CD servicemen who had been given uniforms.

In February 1942, a Defence Regulation was made to 'freeze' part-time volunteers in the CD services. Although a period was given during which persons could leave the service to which they attached, only one or two men in the Decontamination Service did so. The remainder were 'frozen' and thereafter could not leave the service.

During October 1942, large-scale demonstrations using actual mustard gas were held at Northolt, Middlesex. 90 members of the Borough Decontamination Service attended; it was the first time the men had been in actual contact with real mustard gas. Further demonstrations were held in Regent's Park and were also well attended.

In January 1943, the Minister of Labour directed 50 men to the Decontamination service for part-time duty. These men came from all walks of life, and after the initial settling down attended lectures and drills with enthusiasm. Until the fly bombs began in June 1944 the 'directees' attended drills and exercises every Tuesday evening, and with regular training these squads became very efficient and there were few absentees. They also attended – voluntarily – various church and other parades.

During the war, the Decontamination and Repair Squads attended, in strength, all the local Civil Defence Parades and turned out on all occasions in a spick and span condition. The occasion of their first parade was the only anxious time I had. About 60 men had volunteered to turn out, but could they march and manoeuvre with any semblance of order? I found on talking to them that a number of the old soldiers in the service had the same qualms. So one morning, just before the parade at 7.30 a.m. they all assembled in St Pancras Gardens and had a private rehearsal, complete with squad drill and kit inspection. The men were enthusiastic and very soon gave a credible performance in marching. After this there was never any need to wonder how they would appear on parade.

Towards the end of 1943, consideration was given to training the decontamination squads in the specialised work of food 'decontamination'. In January, 1944, lectures and training began. This training in the treatment of foodstuffs contaminated by gas ([26], p 72) was an entirely new subject for the men, but in a month or so, they became quite proficient in the various processes.

Training in general decontamination work continued at regular intervals until the fly bombs began in June 1944. (Although early in 1945 a new training programme was arranged, thanks to the Allied Forces on the Continent, it was never begun.)

Fly Bomb incidents necessitated a change in tactics from the point of view of repairs and clearance of debris. Instead of the available men being distributed over several smaller incidents, the whole of the Borough's resources could be concentrated at one large incident.

A system was instituted whereby immediately a message was received during the daytime giving the location of the incident, all men, lorries and plant were recalled from whatever work they were engaged on and sent to the

scene of the occurrence. As a general rule, within half an hour of the fly bomb falling, a proportion of the men were at work clearing debris, and within an hour this nucleus of men was reinforced up to the maximum required. If the incident occurred at night the men reported at daylight, although the motor brooms were often sent out during the night to start clearance, as during this phase of the war, floodlights and car lights could be used to illuminate the scene.

A typical incident was the one in Whitfield Street, at 1 p.m. on 19 June 1944. 140 men, 15 lorries, 2 motor brooms and a mechanical shovel were at work less than an hour after the bomb dropped. Tottenham Court Road, Goodge Street and Percy Street were covered in broken glass, brickwork, etc., but within two hours the main roadways were cleared and completely opened to traffic; several adjoining roads were also cleared.

The actual damage to roads and sewers

26 Food Treatment Squads; Food Decontamination (Millfield Lane)
Fortunately, poison gas was not used by the Germans, but local authorities had to prepare for that eventuality – this photograph shows Food Decontamination being practised on the Highgate side of Hampstead Heath.

was not a particularly serious problem in these incidents unless the bomb actually fell on the roadway. The clearance of debris in these incidents was, however, quite arduous, as the area of blast damage was very wide. For many days after an incident 30 or 40 men, 6 or 8 lorries and the motor brooms were kept busy clearing the debris as it was put out in the street by householders, and then engaged on first aid repair to houses (O/C, Mr E Winchester). The amount of debris removed during these incidents must have amounted to many thousands of tons. During these large incidents the men turned their hand to all sorts of jobs, one of which was assisting in the removal of furniture from damaged houses.

This résumé would not be complete without reference to the District Foremen, who from February 1940 until the end of the war did regular nights of duty at Inverness Street Depot, so as to be available for any emergency. Also the women sweepers deserve mention for their work of clearing debris; they shovelled and swept as well as any of the men. A word should also be said about the Council's cartage contractors, who, throughout the war, kept us supplied with lorries, often at a few minutes' notice, and in numbers that were far in excess of even the greatest peace-time demands.

In conclusion, I would like to take this opportunity of expressing my appreciation of the help and advice so freely given at all times on matters affecting Decontamination and Repair Services by the Controller, Mr C S Bainbridge. No matter how busy and worried he was, he always found time to attend to matters affecting 'his' men.

Salvage of Goods and Personal Property

Salvage Officers Captain L Sparks, then Cllr C Allen Newbery and others

Rescue of Goods, Furniture and Chattels from Bombed Buildings

On 3 August 1940 the Ministry of Home Security gave directions to local authorities regarding the salvage of property from premises damaged by enemy action. On 9 September instructions were given to designate an officer to be responsible to salvage such personal property and to store it pending its removal by the owner, and on 11 September authority was given to secure premises for the storage of furniture. However, the primary responsibility for recovering and protecting removable goods and articles rested with the *owner*.

The first bombs fell on St Pancras on Sunday 8 September 1940, and for some days furniture was left lying about the streets. The MOH soon got a scheme going and two furniture stores were opened in September, one of which was destroyed a month later. Other stores were soon taken over, and the number of removal vans was increased – the Salvage Department had found its feet.

Early in October Captain L Sparks acted as Removals Officer on behalf of the Chief Warden and in December was officially appointed Removals Officer. Early in September Miss Park started the Personal Property Department (p 76) with an office at the Town Hall, and took charge of handbags, policies, etc., recovered from the debris or found near the incident. On 1 March 1941, Mr C Allen Newbery was appointed Salvage Officer in charge of the Department, Captain Sparks looking after removals and Miss Park all personal property.

March and April saw the two biggest raids on London, and the Salvage department was expanded. Damaged houses were divided into categories: **A**, totally destroyed; **B**, to be demolished; **C**, uninhabitable but capable of repair; **D**, habitable and capable of repair. Furniture could be removed and taken to store only from homes that were uninhabitable.

Owners could arrange private removal and storage to any address in the London region, the Council paying up to £5 for removal expenses on production of a receipt from the removal firm, or by obtaining an official order from the Salvage Officer.

The work of salvaging homes was one that required careful handling; operations would not start until all casualties had been removed. Owners, if present, would often be dazed and unable to make up their minds what to do. Some wanted to remain in the damaged houses and would not move out until a danger notice was placed on their premises, while others would just go away and leave everything. Generally speaking, work would commence on very badly damaged houses where furniture could be moved that was not touching any wall or supporting a damaged ceiling, always provided that the staircase was safe and that authority was given to enter by the senior Rescue Officer present. It often happened that furniture could not be moved until the demolition contractors came to demolish the house weeks or even months afterwards. Many risks were taken by the salvage officers when they went to remove personal property from badly damaged buildings; the Rescue Services often helped by removing furniture from buildings that the salvage staff were not allowed to enter.

Most people were very grateful for any assistance given, but some had no notion of the difficulties. After a big raid it would be many days before the whole area could be cleared. It was impossible for the police to give adequate protection during the blackout, and many things disappeared during the night. In storage and under Home Office Regulations, the contents of drawers, wardrobes or parcels were not the Council's responsibility. Inventories of goods leaving bombed premises were taken under difficult conditions, and a complete list was impossible. A large number of gold watches, clocks and valuable stamp collections were claimed as missing but as a matter of fact, any article of special value found during the move or at the stores was handed to the Personal Property Department at the Town Hall. Some people would move to the country immediately after a raid, return to St Pancras four years later and expect to find a complete home in store.

In 1940 the new staff recruited to the Department had no experience of furniture storage work, but soon settled down, although record-keeping was poor at first. Stacking furniture is a job requiring a lot of experience. Two or three vans might unload at dusk, the furniture could not be properly stacked until next day and the stacks got mixed up, especially if three or more families were living in the same house. When this happened, families were asked to come to the store to sort out their goods, which were then arranged in proper stacks. All goods were listed and marked by streets, not by name. Furniture of any value was salvaged and kept in store for over a year. If no claimant turned up, and the goods were of no appreciable value, they were disposed of. After most raids a lot of furniture, beds, bedding, clothing, etc., was found in the street. These goods were taken to a special store to be sorted into types, then the people who lived in that area were asked to call (all at the same time) to identify their goods. This usually proved satisfactory, and disputed ownership was rare. All unclaimed books were inspected by the Borough librarian; some were selected for use in the Council Library, while others were distributed among the public shelters, the remained being sold for pulping.

The Council provided removal vans through the Highways Department, and on every occasion were able to find some kind of vehicle that was adequate. The salvage department provided their own porters, augmented when required by men from the Highways Department. In June 1941, after the two biggest raids on London, the Salvage Staff at the Town Hall reached its highest level, and consisted of 4 Salvage Officers, 3 Personal Property Officers, 3 Removals staff, 18 Storemen and 12 Porters (total, 40 staff).

During July 1941 the Department was reorganised. One floor at Pratt Street stores was kept for personal property such as bedding, clothing etc. A Salvage Corps of six lorries was formed. The drivers and porters were issued with Salvage Armlets, and given special training. New Furniture Inventory Books were printed in triplicate, and the Wardens' Service was made responsible for taking the inventory. This would be taken as the goods were loaded on to the furniture van, the top copy being given to the owner or sent to him/her later, the second copy to the furniture store, and the third copy remained in the Warden's Book. Captain Sparks left the Department in October 1941. Of the 561 homes in store on 1 January 1942, 223 were in the Euston Street store, 50 in Osnaburgh Street, 110 in Cleveland Street, 120 in Wybert Street and 58 in Pratt Street. In September 1942 the Town Hall salvage staff was reduced to 3 and the storekeepers to 6.

In October 1943 an incident occurred at Birkenhead Street, the first HE incident since May 1941. All the major damage was done in one street and was cleared up satisfactorily with assistance from St Marylebone. The time between the two raids was occupied in clearing old damaged properties and checking the owners of goods in store. In March 1944 heavy bombing took place at Chelsea and Hammersmith, and the Salvage Officer told the Controller he would not be able to cope single-handed with that type and degree of damage if it occurred in St Pancras; as a consequence Mr W D Greenhill was appointed as Assistant Salvage Officer on 5 May 1944. On the night of 15/16 June the first fly bomb fell in St Pancras, and a further 13 by the end of July.

On 15 June the Salvage Department had only two furniture stores, with one storeman in each and no porters. The Town Hall salvage staff consisted of Mr Newbery, Mr Greenhill and Miss Farmer, and Miss Park in charge of personal property. All Hallows Hall, Lyndhurst Hall, St Bede's Hall and Christchurch Hall were taken over as temporary Furniture Stores. Accommodation was later found on the six floors of Fiona House, plus part of the Pharmaceutical Society building in Brunswick Square; this new space sufficed until the end of the war, and the temporary Halls were de-requisitioned in November 1945. The Highways Department, Light Rescue Service and the National Fire Service gave valuable assistance in loading removal vans, and a number of labourers were engaged as porters from the Ministry of Labour. ARP Headquarters assisted by allowing three of their staff to join the salvage department for a few months. Instructors Barnard and Slocombe acted as Salvage Incident Officers and Mr S Nunny

from the Fire Guard Staff assisted in the Salvage Office at the Information Centre.

At one time in July the Salvage Department was working on 7 incidents simultaneously. Salvage Incident Officers were on site from 8 a.m. until after 9 p.m., then returning to the Town Hall with reports. The four Salvage Officers (Newbery, Greenhill, Barnard and Slocombe) were on duty in the Control Room every fourth night, ready to visit any new incident immediately and make the necessary arrangements to deal with it.

At the Brunswick Square and Fiona House stores, hoist lifts were installed after much havering from London Region. They saved the porters from carrying furniture up three or four flights of stairs. Inventory taking proved difficult as it was not always possible to arrange for Wardens to attend.

Between 1 June and 31 December 1945, 429 homes were taken into store, 261 homes were removed from store and 375 homes were moved direct to new addresses. During this period 574 people visited the Salvage Office at the Town Hall, and 815 called at the Salvage Office at the Information Centre. Most of the damage done by the V1 and V2 bombs was in poor districts. Some of the streets were frankly slums, and would have already been demolished had it not been for the war. In a few cases the houses were verminous and in deplorable condition, and in most of them two or three families lived in one house, sometimes in one room. This made removals more difficult. In December 1944, extra staff were engaged to clean and restack furniture. Owners calling to collect their chattels were delighted to see their furniture looking like new.

After a raid we had to advise people who had lost their homes just what to do, explain what the Council could do to assist them, how to make a claim to the District Valuer and so on, which gave distressed folk a lot of comfort; a word of sympathy helped a lot. Some had a very heavy burden to carry. One soldier, a lad of 19, was called back from the Army to find that his family had been wiped out – mother, father, brother, sister. He had to identify their bodies, go through their personal belongings and sort his own out from a mass of goods collected from the incident.

The goods in the Council's furniture

stores on 31 August 1945 were: 134 stacks in the Euston Street building, 103 in Brunswick Square, 97 in Osnaburgh Street and 16 in Fiona House (total, 350 stacks). For the large majority, the names and addresses of the owners are known. All are welcome to remove their goods when they can find a home to put them. Unless new regulations are made regarding the disposal of stored chattels, it looks as though furniture storage will be required in St Pancras for some years to come.

Salvage of Personal Property
Officer in Charge Miss A G Park

A department to salvage personal property was set up at the Town Hall in mid-September 1940 with Miss A G Park in charge. The property was usually recovered from the debris of houses either severely damaged or completely demolished and was therefore usually very dirty, the writing on documents and papers being sometimes almost illegible. As most of the occupants of these houses were severely injured, much of the property remained unclaimed for long periods until the owners were discharged from hospital.

At the site of the incident, personal property would be put in the care of the local Warden, who would take an inventory of the goods retrieved and send them with an accompanying list to the Town Hall, where the articles were checked by *two* persons, with fuller descriptions entered into a ledger; the articles were labelled and stored in a strong room or store room according to their value. All cash – small or large sums – was paid into the Council's Bank, exact records being kept as to where and how the sums were found, payments being made by cheque or cash when the claimants came forward. After the heavy raid in May 1941, over 100 handbags were handed in. Each one had to be examined and a list made of its contents (an extraordinary number of articles were found in most).

In June 1941 a change was made. Personal property was divided into two classes – A: money, handbags, silver articles, jewellery, insurance policies, bank and pension books, medals, ration cards, national registration cards, insurance cards, legal documents and articles of special value; B: clothes, underclothes, hats, bedding, boots and shoes, china, glass, cutlery, ironmongery, carpets, rugs, books, etc. After an incident the Salvage Officer or his deputy would take to the Wardens' Post two or three kitbags. The Post Warden, after listing all the Class A goods, would lock these in one or more kitbags and retain the key. The kitbags would be collected by the Salvage Officer or his deputy, who would take them to the Town Hall and hand them in to Miss Park, who had duplicate keys of all bags, and would lock them up in the strong room until they could be checked and listed. Sometimes as many as six kitbags would be handed in on one day, representing an enormous amount of work of sorting by experienced people. Class B goods were collected and listed on a special form and taken to a furniture store where one floor was retained for this class of goods. A large amount of clothing, bedding etc., would be found in the street, the best being taken to the store, the remainder disposed of.

Persons claiming money or valuables that had belonged to deceased persons had to produce Letters of Administration in respect of the property or estate, and where a Will existed this had to be Proved before the property in question could be handed over. This all involved a considerable amount of correspondence with Solicitors and Probate Officers, and the preparation of statements and specially worded forms of receipt applicable to each case. When the value of the estate was below a certain figure, the Probate Officer was able to obtain a Grant of Administration for the claimants without their having to make application to Somerset House, which saved time and trouble, especially for people who were unused to dealing with business and legal formalities.

It was also necessary to consult the Ministry of Pensions with regard to children orphaned as a result of air raids, as any property to which they were entitled could be handed over only to the guardian appointed by the Ministry.

A major difficulty in identifying owners of property was that so many people have so many things so much alike, cutlery especially, which we examined with a magnifying glass to find hallmarks and maker's names.

During the lull period the Department was fully occupied in tracing not only the owners of unclaimed property, but the present addresses of people formerly resident in the bombed houses. After the incident at Byron Court we sent letters to 51 people, which produced 36 replies and a large number of items claimed. Three or four years would sometimes elapse before owners turned up to ask if anything had been recovered. They might identify some goods that belonged to somebody else who lived in the same house, and be able to give their new address. Many people failed to notify their change of address because they believed that 'the Town Hall would know where they were from their Registration Cards' – not knowing that this information is confidential and not available even to the Council's Officers.

A quotation from one of the Reports on Personal Property gives some idea of the work involved. In the first 7 weeks of the fly-bomb period 60 kitbags of personal property were handed in, plus 12 large articles (wireless sets, typewriter, etc.). Over 200 enquiries were made, and the property of 139 persons handed over to the owners or claimants, but the large number of fatal casualties during the period made handing over most of this property prolonged and difficult. There was cash from 67 persons, of whom 36 had died. Letters of Administration were required for 25 estates, the remaining 7 being dealt with by the Probate Office. Three large sums of money totalling £1657 were received, and the total of small amounts (from shillings to £35) was £450.

The work took a lot of time and worry, but it was always worth it. People returned after a long lapse of time to find in safe custody some cherished possession that might be of no great value but whose recovery brought much joy to the owner.

Food Conservation and Decontamination Service

Officer in Charge Mr S W Capel, assisted by Mr R N Thomas

n December 1939 the Minister of Home Security and the Minister of Food called on Local Authorities to set up a service to deal with foodstuffs contaminated by poison gases through enemy action. The main objects were:

a. To examine and test suspected or contaminated foodstuffs.

b. To salvage for human consumption or other purposes the largest possible quantity of food exposed to the action of poison gas, and

c. To ensure the destruction of contaminated food which had been rendered unfit or unsuitable for any subsequent use.

By 1940 the enemy had used every means in its power except the use of war gases to diminish our supplies of food. Ships, docks, warehouses and other food storage places had been attacked, though not by gas. However, there was no guarantee that gas would not be used.

An appeal was made to food traders in the Borough asking for men to volunteer for this particular activity. Recruiting presented one great difficulty as it had to be done secretly in order not to alarm the public and without any forceful or popular appeal behind it. Most of the eligible men were already doing some form of National Service. However, sixty volunteers were eventually obtained, with reserves. They were trained in anti-gas measures and food testing techniques. Trained men who left their place of work or were called up had to be replaced, and over 100 volunteers were trained in the course of the war. Squads were, as far as possible, formed so as to cover every part of the Borough.

The Open-Air School at Holly Court, Merton Lane, was equipped as a Food Decontamination Site and the site was made ready for receiving large quantities of food. A reserve site was earmarked at Coram's Fields. It was made suitable but not equipped. Practical exercises were held at the Drill Hall (Camden High Street), on food premises and at the Food

Decontamination Site. The whole of the organisation, from top to bottom, was on a voluntary basis; at no time were there any paid personnel.

Because large quantities of foodstuffs are handled and stored in the many railway premises throughout the Borough, contact was made with the railway companies' representatives, and several days were spent inspecting miles of railway lines, sidings and goods yards looking for suitable sites that could provide temporary accommodation for large amounts of contaminated food.

At that time about 1000 catering establishments in the Borough had been licensed by the Ministry of Food – only one type of food premises that had to be reckoned with.

Happily, it has never been necessary to call the Food Treatment squads into action, but we are confident that had the need arisen they would have been fully capable of conserving the food stocks upon which the life of the nation depended. The following extract from a Ministry of Food Circular issued to Local Authorities on this service reads:

The Minister is conscious that this result has been attained only by the ungrudgingly voluntary support and effort of the officers of the Local Sanitary Authorities throughout the Kingdom and the men and women who willingly undertook duties the performance of which would have involved danger and discomfort. In particular, the Minister appreciates the splendid way in which, at the inception of the Service, men and women of the food trades, many of them past middle age, spontaneously offered their services, determined to do their share in safeguarding the food supplies of the nation.

Food damaged by enemy action

The two Food Inspectors also did considerable work with regard to the inspection, sorting, examination and salvaging of foods contaminated by glass splinters, dust etc. Following every bombing incident, the two officers inspected all food premises near the incident. Affected foods were either treated on the spot or removed by the Ministry of Food Salvage Division or the local salvage organisation, according to type and amount. Food too badly damaged to be salvaged was destroyed. The quantity of foodstuffs removed or destroyed was recorded and certificates were issued to the owners to enable them to get replacements or compensation.

The Mortuary Service

Officer in Charge Mr D Crozier

The Mortuary Service involved carrying out sad duties with great tact and understanding, including interviewing people under the most distressing circumstances. St Pancras's Mortuary Team received the highest praise from hundreds of people who visited the Mortuary in Medburn Street NW1.

The staff consisted of the Superintendent, Deputy Superintendent and six Mortuary Attendants, all of whom were fully trained and could also act as drivers or clerks. The staff had three month's training at the Public Mortuary, Camley Street, under the direction of Sir Bernard Spilsbury, Mr Bentley Purchase and Inspector Wilkinson.

A room was set aside for the identification of bodies, where a bier rested on a special platform, covered with a purple pall. The Council offered to make funeral arrangements and inter the victims in the St Pancras War Graves if desired. The Council also helped to solve financial difficulties, and facilitated applications for pensions by opening a Ministry of Pensions office at the Town Hall. Later on, the Mayor provided wooden coffins for those buried by the Council.

Distressed relatives were given sympathetic care by the mortuary staff. A casualty officer from the Police was in constant attendance at the mortuary, which was of great help in tracing and bringing next of kin to the mortuary without delay. A firm of undertakers in the Borough also attended each day. Care was taken to ensure that the next-of-kin's religious views were respected. The Council provided a photographer to take pictures of casualties who would be difficult or take time to identify. The utmost possible care was taken to establish identity beyond all reasonable doubt. Statistics are given in the Table.

Air raid fatalities, 8.9.1940 to 27.3.1945

Bodies dealt with at mortuary	796
Bodies dealt with at hospital	140
Bodies referred to Coroner	4
Presumed deaths	17
Total	957
Ages Up to and including 5	34
6 to 16	64
17 to 45	510
45 to 60	199
61 years of age and over	150
Total	957
Casualties buried by St Pancras Borough Council	72
Casualties unidentified (including 2 from hospital)	10

Rehousing Service

Officer in charge Mr W J Dale

Rest Centres
E C Blight, Chief Officer of Social Services (LCC) for Rest Centres

One of the biggest problems after a raid was to find accommodation quickly for those rendered homeless or obliged to evacuate their homes because of an unexploded bomb. This latter category of people was not thought of when the Rest Centre organisation was planned, and the number of people so affected was vast.

Up to the summer of 1940 there were three first-line rest centres in St Pancras: the Mary Ward Settlement in Tavistock Place and at Netley Street and Queen's Crescent schools, and two second-line centres at Aldenham and Harmood Street schools. The Government scheme was that suitable buildings, often in use for other purposes, were to be reserved as rest centres if and when required, with sufficient equipment and stores being provided to enable hot drinks and light refreshments to be served. The LCC's Public Assistance department stood ready at the local offices of the Department where they were employed to go and open up whatever centres were necessary. Local residents were also enrolled

as volunteers. As back-up to the first- and second-line centres were third-line centres – church halls and similar buildings – with local teams of voluntary helpers organised, where necessary, by the WVS (Women's Voluntary Services, p 80).

After the first heavy raids on 7 September 1940 and the succeeding days it was evident that more first-line centres had to be provided quickly to accommodate the large number of homeless people who had to remain in the centres for much longer periods than had been anticipated, and St Pancras decided to establish 11 completely equipped and staffed first-line centres, all protected by blast walls and strengthened with steel girders. By December 1940 the first-line centres were fully equipped with 3-tier bunks, facilities for cooking all meals, and entirely self-supporting. After a heavy raid Control would contact the Group Rest-Centre Officer to find out what accommodation was available, as numbers of homeless people would frequently come from another borough just over the border. Over 13,000 homeless people were admitted to the rest centres in St Pancras during the war. The rest centre organisation carried out great work in helping the bombed out over the first few days or even weeks, imparting information regarding all types of assistance available from other services, e.g. Assistance Board, Billeting, Claims, or Furniture removal, making enquiries regarding casualties, and generally assisting in sorting out problems.

Hostels

Those who had had to evacuate their homes because of unexploded bombs remained at the rest centre until the bomb was cleared away; the remainder were transferred to hostels, or as they were sometimes called, Halfway Houses. In St Pancras at one time or another the Rehousing Department operated in fourteen hostels, taking over hotels, boarding houses, a part of the Foundling Hospital headquarters, three other houses in Brunswick Square and the Royal Veterinary College.

Some of the hostels were so comfortable that people were reluctant to leave and go to new homes. In the early days of heavy bombing when the pressure was greatest and much had to be improvised, it was impossible to keep detailed records, but many thousands of people made use of these hostels. The largest of these, the Royal Veterinary College, was also used for the reception and temporary housing of thousands of transferred war workers.

Rehousing

Officer in charge, Mr W J Dale

Rehousing all these people was very difficult, as bombing did not cease until 1945. Families who had occupied a whole house or half a house had to be content with a few rooms, although every effort was made to find what they needed. From the beginning of enemy action to the end of the war, billeting warrants were issued for 8,536 people, and 814 families totalling 2,780 people were rehoused in requisitioned property. During the two years from December 1940 to the end of 1942 most vacancies on the Council's estates were made available to the Rehousing Department for bombed-out families, and 310 families totalling 940 people were rehoused in this way. A further 130 families, totalling 480 people, were rehoused on LCC Housing Estates with the direct assistance of the Rehousing Department. In addition, about 850 families, totalling 2,970 people, were found or helped to find accommodation in privately owned property. Just over 400 requisitioned properties were held by the Department at the end of June 1945, most of them occupied.

The small staff in Rehousing had a difficult job and thankless task, meeting obstacles at every corner, but in spite of it all carried out a wonderful job of work.

Women's Voluntary Services

Mrs D Agnew, WVS Centre Organiser 1938-1945

When I first came to St Pancras at the end of October 1938 Mrs McGougan was the WVS Organiser. Mrs McGougan left London after Christmas and Lady Stewart became Centre Organiser. Miss Stonelake joined us in 1938 and remained throughout the war.

Many women offered to train for auxiliary nursing and the most suitable were asked to interview at the Town Hall in the evenings before a small panel: a Hospital Matron and Lady Stewart or myself. About 100 went through.

We arranged meetings at different Guilds, Social Centres and Clubs to persuade people to train in elementary ARP, dealing with Gas attacks and First Aid. Over 3,000 volunteers enrolled for the various services and branches of women's war work other than the Armed Services, such as NAAFI and CD ambulance drivers. We also started six work parties of about 300 members who made hospital supplies, knitted for the Forces, and made clothes for evacuated children. We sent volunteers to staff canteens in ARP depots and feeding centres at the Mary Ward Settlement, in Netley Street and Queen's Crescent.

Smoothing the evacuation of children outside London was a very big job, which continued throughout the war. Fortunately, Mrs Carroll Marx, with her extensive knowledge of the Borough and fluent French and German, joined us at the outbreak of war. One day we did one of the queerest 'hush-hush' jobs: escorting foreign women refugees from an address in Fulham at 7 a.m. to Liverpool en route to the Isle of Man, where they were to be interned. There were about 50 buses, a lot of police including 5 women, and 10 WVS officers. We went by bus to Addison Road, and got our busloads into the train, with porters kept at a distance. We were locked in with them and went off to Liverpool, where we handed them over and returned that evening to London with a very cheerful party of Metropolitan police who entertained us with a concert all the way home. We arrived at 1 a.m.

In **1940** Lady Stewart started the first **Housewives Service** and enrolled 874 members, who were generally helpful to their neighbours in time of need. As a service it dwindled rather, until it was revived and used much more under the Invasion Defence Scheme and during the fly bomb and V2 period. Lady Stewart addressed 35 women's meetings and spoke to 2,650 schoolchildren on Salvage. We helped at **Play Centres** and did a lot of station **escort work**. Bombing was very heavy. We had staffed six **Third-Line Rest Centres** (see p 79) which were working well. The Clothing Department, now well established, clothed 2,318 people. At this early period of bombing we were asked to help billet the homeless. The billeting was a nightmare, because of the lack of accommodation. The Local Authority had agreed to provide the billets if we would allocate the homeless to them and take them there. In three Green Line buses with a policeman in each, we collected people from the Rest Centres and drove off, hoping to put them into suitable accommodation. Often on arrival we would find the house occupied, badly damaged or otherwise unsuitable

and we had to continue trying to place our mixed loads of large families and old people, generally with air raid warnings going all the time, and only giving up at or after dark. I was impressed with the courage and patience of people who had just suffered the loss of their homes in a bad raid: all behaved calmly and the older ones were magnificent. We dealt with approximately 824 homeless people before the Local Authority took over with proper requisitioning powers and more Rest Centres and Half-Way Houses materialised.

1940 also saw the influx of **foreign refugees**. The Town Clerk asked us to visit areas suitable for billeting, and all through a grilling hot weekend we went in and out of houses in WC1, filling in particulars and explaining why. We listed some 1,400 possible billets. Then we had to meet the first arrivals at St Pancras station. A team with interpreters was there night and day, but soon arrangements were tightened and all refugees had to go to an assembly camp for a few days, and from there in lots of 50 or 100 a day to St Pancras. After discussion with the police we arranged for their reception at the Town Hall.

The refugees arrived in buses under strict supervision and were not allowed to make contact outside. Mrs Carroll Marx allotted billets and I made general arrangements. I had 26 interpreters and on arrival each group was given an interpreter speaking their native language or one they understood. Our canteen served refreshments and we placed their luggage in a corner labelled alphabetically, as they liked to keep an eye on it. The Breton fishing folk, who looked so well with their wholesome tanned faces, posed the biggest problem. One family had sailed over in an open boat, with grandparents, great-grandparents, uncles, aunts and children, and all their worldly goods tied up in bedspreads and tablecloths. Of course none of the party wanted to be detached from their relatives.

The refugees first passed by the billeting table, received identity cards and money if needed, then into the police interviewing room – sometimes detained for a considerable time – on to police photography and finishing with gas masks. The interpreter then handed them over to the escort, who took them by car to the billet, where Mrs Marx had sent a messenger to warn the householder to be ready for them. The next day they came to the office for clothes, help with food, shopping, enquiries for relatives, complaints of the landlady, where to go for medical advice, etc.

Mrs Franklin had a clothing depot specially for refugees. She and Miss Ottewill, and later Mrs and Miss Hurst, did welfare work for them. We had mostly French and Belgian people, and a few Dutch, Polish, Maltese from Marseilles, and Czechs. Later on, an empty country house was taken for some and throughout Mrs Marx and Miss Hurst acted as billeting officers, as they could manage the languages. Most of the Poles went North and rejoined their husbands in the RAF, some of the fisherfolk went back to France. Mrs Franklin arranged English classes, some garden allotments and Christmas parties, and even settled many family disputes.

Our evacuation officer (Hon. Mrs Rea) made an arrangement with the WVS in Hampshire for the **evacuation of old people**, and 108 old people were got away to billets. They used to meet for tea in the afternoons at a club run by three elderly sisters (evacuees). Two or three marriages were arranged there and caused much excitement, the brides and grooms being between 76 and 80. Only two came back to London, one old man who missed his pals and an old lady who missed her evening paper. Later, in the fly-bomb period, many more were sent away through a scheme operated from WVS Headquarters. Some country houses were requisitioned and staffed and the old people were taken down by special train with a canteen and sick-bay on board. Others were taken to institutions arranged by the Ministry of Health.

In May **1941** our office windows and doors were blown in. Lady Stewart left London and Mrs Carroll Marx also left to work with the British Red Cross.

The **Clothing Department** for air raid victims was now well established, and worked very hard. When clothing coupons were introduced much detailed paperwork had to be done for the Board of Trade, and all garments had to be scrupulously listed. The Lord Mayor's Fund, the Colonies and American Red Cross had supplied some lovely clothes, and gifts of second-hand clothes were invaluable, enabling us to give immediate and extra help before people had obtained their coupons. Hundreds of blankets have been given out, and toilet articles such as combs, razors, toothbrushes and shaving cream, which really pleased people; also small needlework cases, torches, shoelaces, braces and hot water bottles. Clothing dumps were opened in five other places, all needing a watchful eye and continual care. There were but few scroungers and grumblers. Up to June 1945 we clothed 9,274 people.

One human story always amuses us: a young woman, her three babies (triplets) and a child of 18 months came for clothes. They were all rigged out in lovely baby clothes and given all they needed; two were to be evacuated and one the mother could manage. The next day we were told that the father was not married to the girl and the children's agency was trying to persuade him to do so, but he said he didn't want to rush into anything in wartime!

Later in the war we had to clothe some repatriated prisoners, with terrible accounts of life in German concentration camps. One man could not find his family and seemed so hopeless and broken. We also clothed an English boy who had been at school in Holland and had been forced to work by the Germans. Now he was back, but his family – parents and brothers – have so far not been traced.

Invasion Defence was organised in 1942. There were miles of checking and re-listing billets, done by 17 helpers. All Third-Line Rest Centres were given extra stores and more staff, and three more were established, at Friends' House, Lyndhurst Hall and Buck Street Presbyterian Church, to accommodate 6,000 people if needed. Rehearsals were held in all of them, and staff allotted to each in Canteen, Welfare, Billeting, Guides to Billets, Stores and Luggage. Luckily this scheme never had to operate, but meanwhile we learned to build outside cooking stoves, and good tests were made in each area of Street Party Leaders and their capabilities.

During the Fly Bomb and V2 period, we staffed **Incident Inquiry Points** day and night for as long as the Incident Officer required it. All enquiries were put on a card index, with all the information on casualties we could get. We still get people making enquiries about relatives and friends from some of the early fly bomb raids. We opened very quickly after an incident in daylight, and Mrs Brockman always drove me off at once, with a helper. Others were telephoned to join us. At night, Control contacted whoever was on call, and she called up a car and picked up her other helpers. We took a broom to sweep the glass away from our Point and an urn to make tea for people waiting for news, or having to be told bad news. After a short time the first Hospital Lists were collected, all information was carded and copies were given to Control, Chief Warden, Police and Incident Officer. The hours were long, and the work was often heartrending, but all were glad to do it and felt it to be very worthwhile.

Mrs Hurst and Mrs Brockman ran a **Comforts and Work Department**. This kept several large work parties supplied with work and wool to be knitted for the Armed Services, chiefly for the WAAFs [Women's Auxiliary Air Force] and ATS [(women's) Auxiliary Territorial Service], Civil Defence and Merchant Navy. Lovely toys were made and given to Wartime Day Nurseries and bombed children, as well as hundreds of overalls made from Ministry of Health material for these nurseries. A large number of private knitters did a lot of work which had to be collected and returned to the proper Depot, and the full weight of wool supplied. Now they are knitting hard for men in Burma and the Far East. 48,709 garments have been completed to date.

From May **1943** we worked with Mr Jones on **rehousing**. At the Information Centre there was always one WVS member, up to 5 of them after a raid, one taking particulars of **personal salvage** and forwarding them to the Personal Property Department (p 76) at the Town Hall. Some helpers worked with Miss Park in that Department after raids.

We ran the **Canteen** for everyone in the Rehousing Department and for all air raid sufferers awaiting their turn for information and attention. Several hundreds of cups of tea a day would be served. From the very early days of the War we staffed the Mobile Canteen. On call night and day, for about two years the volunteers slept every night

at Malet Place. Later, besides air raid work, the Mobile has been going out on Saturdays and Sundays to feed Demolition workers ([24], p 65). We ran several Home Guard canteens and one at a Youth Centre, and many people worked at Service Canteens such as King's Cross Mission, Ashley House, and Euston Canteen.

When in 1942 the Voluntary **Car Pool** was started by the Ministry of Transport it was operated by the WVS, and St Pancras was made the Pool for St Pancras, Islington and Stoke Newington. Using 12 drivers we averaged 1,500 miles per month. More drivers entered the Pool until there were nearly 80, many of these for emergency only, and mileage increased to 4,000 a month. In March 1944 Islington and Stoke Newington Boroughs were detached and we acquired Hampstead. During the fly bomb period the mileage again increased, the peak being reached in July 1944, when 8,000 miles were covered. Apart from post-raid work we supplied cars for all the Ministries, Local Authorities, and nearly every hospital in London. It was a large and very worrying job to get hold of cars when needed to take people after raids to the Rest Centres or Mortuary, and fetching volunteers for Incident Information Points when they had no other means of getting there at night.

The WVS started organising **War Savings** seriously in 1941 with War Weapons Week, when we staffed many small Selling Stations. Later, we were reorganised, and opened a Selling Centre in Camden High Street, staffed by the WVS six days a week. In the first week we took £386 over the counter and in Battleships Week £3,825. In July, 330 streets were covered and we took £2,443 that month over the counter. In March 1943, in 'Wings for Victory' week we took £27,537. Finally, in 'Salute the Soldier' week (June 1945) we took £10,954.15.0

Some other activities are as follows:
Endless Flag days.
Escort work at all hours for Ministry of Labour, meeting the men and women being transferred to different jobs. Big batches of Irishmen to be taken to hostels, taken to get instructions, seen off at stations.
Escort work for young wives of servicemen and their babies on their way from or to Scotland.
Meeting Americans coming over to work and helping them whilst in London for a few days.

Sometimes giving hospitality for a night.

Distributing Belgian toys and buying £50 worth of toys, the gift of the South African Voluntary Services, Johannesburg, to Wartime Nurseries.

Distributing stores of dried milk, cocoa, drinking chocolate and rice to hospitals and institutions.

Clerical help at the Food Office on special occasions.

A rush job of some weeks at the Air Ministry, at the War Office and at the Evening Standard, sorting papers for troops.

Helping at Food and Fuel demonstrations.

Hospital mending.

Hospital domestic work.

Welfare work at the Grafton Hotel for Gibraltarians.

Fifteen volunteers were trained by the Home Guard for signalling, switchboard, Morse code and clerical work.

Supplying 5 people under the care of Provision of Industry for the Physically Handicapped with wool for knitting, and sometimes orders for knitting.

Our last big job was the **Gift and Rehousing Scheme** for the people bombed out during the V1 and V2 periods. The Mayor and the WVS of Halifax adopted St Pancras and sent us 17 tons of furniture – beds, bedding, chairs, tables and other furniture, ornaments, glass and china, lovely cutlery, and household linen. Then Leicester sent 40 tons one morning and we were nearly swamped. It was grand stuff, and with the cooperation and splendid help of Mr Marsh and his men at the Furniture Store it was unloaded and stored. Everything was allocated points – each family in the A and B categories of bombing (p 73) was entitled to 30 points per head in the household and 50 for the house. The less badly bombed categories C and D got 20 per house and 30 per person.

People thought this system fair. We have had many charming and grateful letters. Many too have been sent to Halifax and Leicester. We had about six wireless sets and as I write they are being repaired. One has gone to a very lonely old man, one to a young woman very badly damaged in the face and with one eye gone. By 31 August 1945 we have completed 700 families, and partly finished 60.

Before closing this account of our work I would like to say how grateful I am to the three Mayors, Alderman Evan Evans, Alderman Minter and Alderman Mitchell, under whom I have served, for their help and sympathy. Also to Mr Austin, the Town Clerk, and Mr Bainbridge, the ARP Controller, for their advice and backing if I was in any difficulty. Our work too with the Wardens' Service has been very interesting and very happy these last years. We were fortunate in working with Mr Dale of Rehousing, and also in the War Savings effort. Mr Warne too was very obliging, and although I always seemed to be asking him for something, he generally seemed able to produce it.

Most of all I would like to acknowledge how very much I owe to the people who have worked steadily all through with me; for the unfailing loyalty and self-imposed discipline that these voluntary workers have always shown, regarding their hours of work as definite periods, and courteously telling me if they had to be away, or if ill, sending a Doctor's Certificate. They have all had their own worries and sorrows, and household duties to perform, and in spite of these things have given hours of day and night work to the WVS work. To them must go any credit that may be given to us, and to the prompt and efficient help we have always received from our Group Office.

Note by C A Newbery

The above report of the WVS was prepared by Mrs Dorothy C Agnew, Centre Organiser for St Pancras WVS. Naturally, she has said little about her own work. Mrs Agnew was always well to the fore on any job of work for the WVS; nothing was too much trouble, and she had an extraordinary way of surmounting any difficulty, with a strong determination to overcome any obstruction. Mrs Agnew set a great example of real hard public service, and all the citizens of St Pancras owe her an enormous debt of gratitude.

Bombing statistics 1939-1945

Approximate number of air raid messages and warnings:

Yellow 876   Purple 463   Red 1,136

Approximate number of incidents in the Borough:				1,278
"	"	"	high-explosive bombs	610
"	"	"	parachute mines	14
"	"	"	phosphorus incendiary bombs	2
"	"	"	oil bombs	32
"	"	"	fly bombs	20
"	"	"	long-range rockets	3
"	"	"	unexploded HEs	157
"	"	"	unexploded PMs	5
"	"	"	unexploded PhIBs	6
"	"	"	unexploded oil bombs	2
"	"	"	incendiary bomb incidents, night of 16/17 April 1941	50
"	"	"	incendiary bomb incidents, night of 10/11 May 1941	34
"	"	"	incendiary bomb incidents, altogether a further	<u>343</u>

Total   1,278

Casualties

Approximate number of people killed in the Borough				957
"	"	"	seriously injured and taken to hospital	1,443
"	"	"	minor casualties	<u>3,040</u>

Total   5,440

Damaged Houses

Category	'A' & 'B'	(demolished or to be demolished)	1,576
"	'Ca'	(badly damaged but capable of being repaired)	1,696
"	'Cb'	(uninhabitable – will take some time to repair)	1,744
"	'D'	(blast damage)	<u>13,825</u>

Total   18,841

Index